Relieved of Command

Relieved of Command

Benjamin S. Persons
Captain,
U.S. Public Health Service,
Reserve Inactive

Sunflower University Press®
1531 Yuma • P. O. Box 1009 • Manhattan, Kansas 66505-1009 USA

ISBN 0-89745-204-6

Edited by Julie Bush

Layout by Lori L. Daniel

This book is for

Marydear

*who sent a son to war with a smile on
her face and an ache in her heart*

for

Ellis O. Davis, Jr., Colonel CE, USA

who gave me inspiration, guidance, and orders

and for

Frances Neisler

*who waited for me and was
there when I returned*

Contents

Introduction

BEING FIRED happens all the time and is hardly newsworthy. It is so commonplace in our society that one expects it to happen at least once in a career. Yet, when it happens to a senior military or naval officer during wartime, it is news.

The military Commander who feels the heat from his superior can demonstrate that he is tough and can do something that should please his superior by firing one or several subordinates. Abe Lincoln tried — God knows he tried — to find a Commander who could whip Robert E. Lee during the Civil War. Five times he was to drink the bitter tea, going through the aging Winfield Scott, Irvin McDowell (brevet major of the Adjutant General Department), George McClellan (who wouldn't fight but chose to remain in bivouac making plans), A. E. Burnside and George G. Meade (who together deserve no more than a listing), and finally Ulysses S. Grant (who met Lee at Appomattox).

Though Intelligence was probably withheld from Admiral Husband E. Kimmel and General Walter C. Short prior to the bombing of Pearl Harbor in 1941, they were both found to have been negligent in not posting someone or something out there to give a little warning that the "Japs were coming." They were both sacked.

Major General Lloyd R. Fredendall, Commander of the II ("two eye") U.S. Army Corps at the Battle of Kasserine Pass in 1943, was sacked for failure to prepare properly for an attack and for failure to defend adequately the key rear position critical to the safety of a corps on his flank.

Lieutenant General Mark Clark, Commander of the 5th Army in Italy in 1944, "relieved" his close friend, Major General John P. Lucas, the Field Commander at Anzio, ostensibly because Lucas was exhausted. Actually, it was because Winston Churchill, who always had a fondness for "the soft underbelly of Europe," was disappointed in the progress of the war on the Italian peninsula and demanded a head. The choice was Lucas, Clark, or Dwight D. Eisenhower, and the reader could have predicted the result.

Major General Alan W. Jones of the ill-fated 106th Infantry Division, which suffered the greatest defeat of any American military force in history, was "relieved of command" in December 1944 when his command no longer existed — less than three weeks after he first committed his troops to combat.

General Joseph W. "Joe" Stilwell was sacked because he thought Chiang Kai-shek was "an ass" and publicly said so.

General Douglas MacArthur used every means at his disposal to provoke President Harry Truman to relieve him so that he, MacArthur, would not have to face the indignity of the inevitable stalemate in Korea. Much to his credit, Truman finally obliged.

In this monograph, I have attempted to tell of several who were "relieved of command" — both a routine rostering change of command or, as more commonly thought, a pejorative action. These stories are all different. In some, the results could have been foreseen; in others, the relief was unexpected.

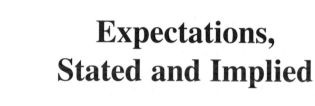

Chapter 1

Expectations,
Stated and Implied

*T*HE OSTENSIBLE *intent of a military mission is to further the stated or implied goal of the entity that sent the mission out. Soldiers take to the field to do what they believe the king wants of them.*

After receiving the grand commission, the newly appointed Commander sets about recruiting a force, making arrangements to clothe, feed, arm, and train the new muster, stocking the finance officer with sufficient coin to pay the troops, and generally preparing for that day when in the early morning mist the enemy is first sighted. Meanwhile, somewhere in the world, the Commander has a counterpart, an adversary whom he will someday meet in battle. Their missions, interestingly, are not dissimilar.

Communications are almost always from the top down ("You do this") and from the bottom up ("This is what I have done"). It is seldom that the one issuing orders will tolerate being told what the subordinate believes to have heard his orders to be. In battle, carrying out orders is measured by success. If you do not take the hill that I have commanded you to take, then you have not carried out my orders and, perhaps, you have even disobeyed me. I may choose to excuse your failure and give you other orders to carry out, or I may simply tell you again to take the hill. If those who give me orders are critical of my accomplishments, I may relieve you of your command and try to find someone who can and will take the hill. But then *"less than success, but worthy effort"* is often judged by how many men you have lost in the trying. Nineteenth-century Field Marshal Helmuth Karl Bernhard von Moltke is reputed to have said that a general officer is never really seasoned until he has lost a whole division. But it is not this simple. Confederate General Joseph E. Johnston was sacked on July 17, 1864, for not fighting the Yankees and keeping his army; his successor, Lieutenant General John Bell Hood, was sacked for fighting and losing his army.

The significant ingredient is success. Neither Johnson nor Hood were successful. On the other hand, General Robert E. Lee was, and history has treated him kindly. As the adage goes, "Success begets success."

Perhaps more important is public image. Few knew this better than Douglas MacArthur and Dwight D. Eisenhower, who operated their very lives under the council of publicity and image and had staffs who saw to it that the great leaders were always pictured in the most flattering light. Because it is hardly popular to sack one who is immensely admired, safety comes in keeping up the public image. During the midst of the Yalu River crisis in 1950, which finally cost MacArthur his corncob pipe, most Americans sided with MacArthur and thought we should bomb past the Yalu, even up to and including attacking Peking with the atomic bomb. Fortunately, President Harry S. Truman sensed the peril of a ground war with China and avoided this by affirming the policy of protecting South Korea and Formosa and no more.

Of equal importance with success is the Commander's willingness to

Relieved of Command				
Reliever	**Commander**[1]	**Unit**	**Location**	**Date**
Eisenhower	**Fredendall**	II Corps	Kasserine	March 1943
Kincaid, USN	**Brown, A.**	7th Division	Aleutians	May 1943
Bradley	**Allen & Roosevelt**	1st Division	Sicily	July 1943
Clark	**Lucas**	VI Corps	Anzio	February 1944
Bradley	**Bohn**	CCB 3rd Armored Division	Normandy	June 1944
Bradley	McMahon	8th Division	Normandy	June 1944
Collins	**McKelvie**	90th Division	Normandy	June 1944
Smith, H.M.	**Smith, R.**	27th Division	Saipan	June 1944
Bradley	**Landrum**	90th Division	Normandy	July 1944
Bradley	Brown, L.	28th Division	Normandy	August 1944
Bradley	Silvester, L.	7th Armored Division	Ruhr	October 1944
Bradley	Corlett	XIX Corps	Ruhr	October 1944
Patton	Wood	4th Armored Division	Rhine	December 1944
Ridgway	**Jones**	106th Division	Bulge	December 1944
Hodges	Millikin	III Corps	Remagen	March 1945

[1] Bold-faced entries cited within.

accept a pragmatic shift in stated purpose/policy, which may not result in coincidence with the policy of the Commander. Neither MacArthur, Truman, nor the United Nations had a clear idea of what was to be done in Korea more than forcing the North Koreans to give up what they had taken. As circumstances began to favor the United Nations and the United

States, MacArthur began thinking of punishing the North Koreans and, maybe, slightly punishing the Chinese for helping the North Koreans. Truman, who had declined the offer of Chinese Nationalist troops, began to sense, as the North Koreans were being driven back from whence they came, that if we pushed too far, we would find ourselves in a shooting war with China. Hence, our stated policy was subtly changed to "recover the land we lost, but don't provoke the Chinese to war." MacArthur began saying, "There is no substitute for victory." Truman thought that peace was worth substituting. And that's all it took.

It is probably safe to assert, though rather cynically, that the Commander expects of the subordinate what his mind tells him to expect at the moment, regardless of whether or not the subordinate knows what is expected of him. Here reality or fantasy become important. The successful beleaguered Commander recognizes his assets and liabilities and operates within the limitations these impose. The Commander who fantasizes of being rescued by mythical armies, as Hitler did in the last days in Berlin in 1945, is — to quote 19th-century German military theorist Karl von Clausewitz — "a fool." Contrast the fool with one who orders a rescue effort to be made by a force about which the orderer knows everything: location, strength, fighting ability. Reality diminishes impossible odds. Remember the besieged 12th-century crusade force that, having eaten the last rat in the encircled Turkish city, marched out to meet the enemy, who outnumbered them three to one, and handily whipped the hell out of them. The outcome was at best unlikely, nigh on to impossible, but the action began from reality.

Let us, therefore, put a few of these sacked Commanders under the scrutiny of the hand lens. What follows is a fragmentary listing of combat-command general officers who were relieved while commanding brigades, combat commands, divisions, or corps. These will serve to illustrate that relief of a subordinate, though not commonplace, did happen.

Chapter 2

Harding on the Trail Through Hell

*E*DWIN F. HARDING *was born in Franklin, Ohio, in 1886. He graduated from the U.S. Military Academy at West Point, New York, in 1909, and married Eleanor Hood in 1913. He was commissioned a second lieutenant, U.S. Infantry, in 1909 and attended the Infantry School at Fort Benning, Georgia (1928), the Command and General Staff School at Fort Leavenworth, Kansas (1929), and the Army War College at Carlisle Barracks, Pennsylvania*

General George C. Marshall congratulating Major General Edwin F. Harding after having presented him with the Legion of Merit for outstanding service as Commanding General of Panama Mobile Forces & Antilles. (U.S. Signal Corps)

Opposite: *From Papuan Campaign: The Buna-Sanananda Operation, 16 November 1942 - 23 January 1943* (Washington, D.C., Center of Military History, U.S. Army, 1990)

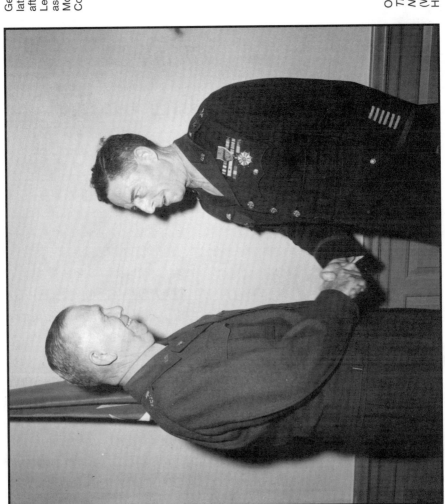

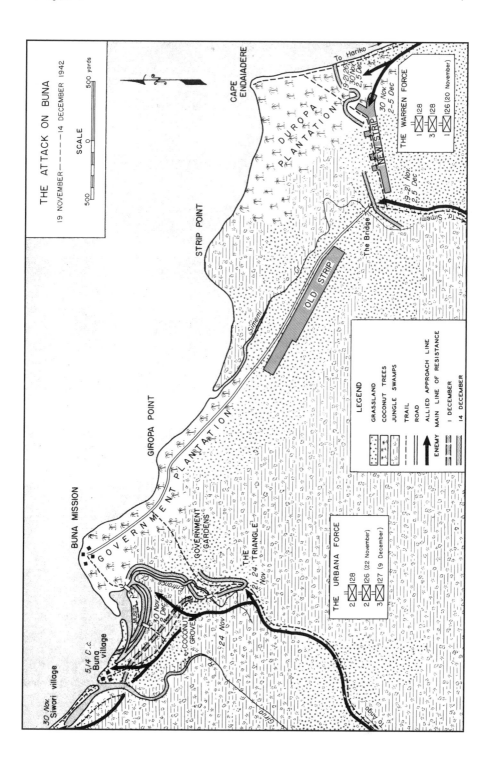

THE ATTACK ON BUNA
19 NOVEMBER——————14 DECEMBER 1942

SCALE
500 0 500 yards

LEGEND
GRASSLAND
COCONUT TREES
JUNGLE SWAMPS
TRAIL
ROAD
ALLIED APPROACH LINE
ENEMY MAIN LINE OF RESISTANCE
1 DECEMBER
14 DECEMBER

THE WARREN FORCE
1 128
3 128
1 126 (20 November)

THE URBANA FORCE
2 128
2 126 (22 November)
3 127 (9 December)

CAPE ENDAIADERE
DUROPA PLANTATION
To Hariko
19-21 Nov, 26, 30 Nov 2,5 Dec
30 Nov 2-5 Dec
NEW STRIP
19-21 Nov 2,5 Dec
To Simemi
The Bridge
STRIP POINT
OLD STRIP
Simemi
GIROPA POINT
GOVERNMENT PLANTATION
BUNA MISSION
GOVERNMENT GARDENS
THE "TRIANGLE"
21,24 Nov
24 Nov
MUSITA
30 Nov 2 Dec
COCONUT GROVE
5/4 C.C. Buna village
30 Nov Siwori village
To Ango
Girua

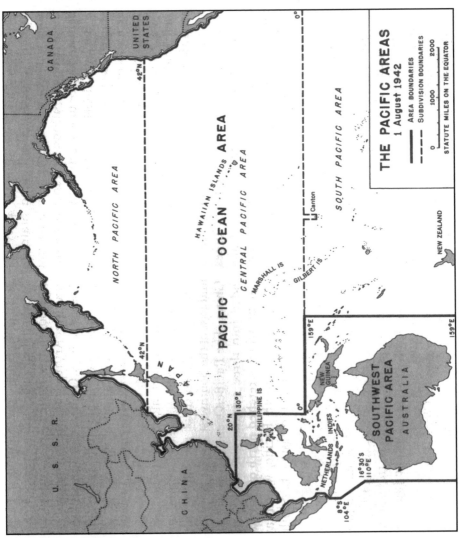

From *U.S. Army in World War II: The War in the Pacific, Seizure of the Gilberts and Marshalls*, by Phillip A. Crowl and Edmund G. Love (Washington, D.C.: U.S. Army, Office of the Chief of Military History, 1955), 6.

*(1929). He was on the faculty at the Military Academy from 1919 to 1923 and the Infantry School from 1929 to 1933 and was the associate editor of the **Infantry Journal** from 1934 to 1938. He commanded the 27th Infantry in Hawaii from 1938 to 1940, was Assistant Division Commander of the 9th Division in 1941, and commanded the 32nd Division in New Guinea during the most arduous phase of the campaign. He commanded the Panama Canal Mobile Force in 1943 and 1944 and the Antilles Department in 1944 and 1945. He directed the Historical Division of the Office of the Chief of Staff from 1945 until his retirement in 1946. For his action in New Guinea in 1942 he received the Silver Star. He retired in 1946 at his permanent rank of major general. He died in 1970 and is buried in Franklin, Ohio.*

In the spring of 1942, the euphoria that came from the unbroken and uninterrupted string of Japanese successes led to bitter debates between the army and navy of Japan as to which was the better course of action — to continue occupying strategic islands that could be used to interdict supply of larger land masses, or simply to occupy these large land masses. The land mass in question was the continent of Australia. By early 1943, the Allies were losing the Philippines, Malaysia, and Burma, and the Japanese were threatening Trincomalee in Ceylon (Sri Lanka) and seriously talking about landing on the north coast of Australia and taking the whole country. It was thought among Japan's strategic planners that the occupation of the land mass would, according to the Japanese navy estimate, require five divisions, while the army believed that to capture the whole of Australia would require 12 divisions, take months, and tie up a million tons of shipping.

It is interesting to note the disparity between the Japanese army and the navy as to the number of army divisions required to wrest Australia from its inhabitants. The navy, believing it would be a "piece of cake" to take Australia, could point to the fact that most of the Australian army was away in the Middle East and could not be brought home in time to have an influence in the land campaign. In addition, the navy could recount the success and ease with which it had bombed Port Moresby, New Guinea, for the first time on February 3, 1943, from its newly acquired base in Rabaul, New Britain, in the Solomons. The 600-mile bombing run from

Rabaul to Port Moresby was done efficiently with the Zero fighter-bomber A6M Mitsubishi, which carried one 250-pound bomb and was armed with two 20-mm cannons and two 7.7-mm machine guns. There was little resistance in Port Moresby to the Mitsubishi.

The Japanese effort in this part of the Pacific was comprised of the South Seas detachment under the command of Major General Tomitaro Horii and consisted of the crack 155th Infantry Regiment, fresh from the mainland of China and a string of successes down to its present base in New Britain. It was supported by the veteran 15th Engineer Regiment, commanded by Colonel Yosuke Yokoyama, which also had seen service in China and later in Malaysia. Vice Admiral Shigeyoshi Inouye was the navy commander. He had to his credit the capture of Guam, though this had not been such an accomplishment. (The most spirited engagement at Guam had resulted in less than 20 casualties, both sides combined. The one American boat that could and did fight was an old tug/utility ship that was steam-powered.) The admiral had at his disposal sufficient transport to move the army troops, his company of marines, the 5th Sasebo Special Naval Land Force (SNLF), and also the supporting troops that the army had in order to augment the capability of the foot soldiers — that is, medium and light artillery, mobile anti-aircraft and service units, including mule quartermaster supply units. These latter would serve well in New Guinea and would be parroted by the Americans who, before it was finished, would resort to most any means of transporting food, ammunition, and wounded. Transportation became so critical that the moving of the dead became a second priority.

New Guinea is an interesting island. A cursory examination of the configuration of the land mass reveals that at one time it could have fit nicely into the continent of Australia, which is the current postulation of geomorphologists. It is thought that the geographic divorce occurred during the Pleistocene epoch, by geologic standards not too long ago — only a few million years! On the island are three distinct land regions; in this regard it is not unlike the state of Tennessee. To the west lies the Vogelskopf (birdshead) peninsula. Along the north of this region are three volcanic mountains that soar to heights of 16,000 feet. In the south, surrounding the indentation in the island filled by the Arafura Sea, are lowlands. The Digul and Fly Rivers, which empty to the south, form a peninsula. To the east of 143 degrees, volcanoes reappear, though their tops are of lesser elevation than those of the west. The island, lying just below the equator, is tropical. The coastal soils support the abundant growth of the tenacious and pernicious kunai, or spear grass, which grows densely and has sharp edges that cut. This grass furnished ideal conceal- ment for the Japanese defenders but was an impedance to the Allied at- tackers.

Japan began its Pacific adventure with the United States on Decem- ber 7, 1941, and by mid-spring, it was invincible. It had come roaring over from the west to take Wake Island and down from the north to take the Philippines and the Marianas. Farther west, it had taken Malaya and the invincible fortress of Singapore. The Netherlands East Indies had fallen in spite of the best showing yet by a fighting force of the Allies — that of the gallant Dutch navy, which had dealt the Japanese a blow or two and had come away with some of its ships still able to fight. Getting ever closer to one of its prizes, Australia, the Japanese conquered with ease the Aus- tralian territory islands of New Britain, the lesser-known New Ireland, and the completely unknown islands of Guadalcanal and Bougainville in the Bismarck archipelago.

On July 22 and 23, 1942, the forces of Major General Tomitaro Horii, aboard the naval convoy of their two transports protected by two light cruisers and three destroyers, made the landing area of deep water off Dyke Acland Bay near Sanananda Point, New Guinea, and there debarked their cargo of troops and equipment. There was no one to meet them with any resistance. After making an effort to establish some semblance of a base at the trading village of Buna, they made for the south. Their goal was the capture of Port Moresby, which is actually to the southwest, but one must first go south along the trail that crosses the formidable Owen Stan- ley Range.

Although the Japanese were fiercely attacked by the U.S. Army Air Forces during the landings, more than 11,000 combat soldiers and their supplies, weapons, and vehicles were landed over the course of several days. Immediately they made their way to the mountains and struck up- ward and westward over them on the Kokota Trail — a winding, muddy forest track with many switchbacks that alternately gains or loses altitude. The Japanese marched unopposed over the trail to a point 32 miles from Port Moresby, where they were stopped by Australian defenders. They were unceremoniously driven back up the mountain and down its north slope. The pursuing Australians wisely waited to attack while they called on the central command in the Pacific. General Douglas MacArthur, learning of this and not being content to leave it as an Australian problem, decided that the Japanese should immediately be thrown off the island. It could be argued that the tiny Japanese occupying force, really but an enclave where the landing had been made, could best be served by encapsulating them, setting a perimeter around them, cutting off their supply from the sea, and simply letting them starve. But such reason does not pervade the minds of military men. If investment were an option, there would never have been a Corregidor nor a Masada.

Meanwhile, the Japanese, perhaps intent on getting ready to invade Australia or on diverting Allied attention away from Guadalcanal, determined to establish a foothold elsewhere on New Guinea. In late August, while the Japanese attackers were still south of the Owen Stanleys, more Japanese landed in Milne Bay with a force of about battalion size. They were met almost at the beach by the Australians, who spoiled their intent of surprise. Three days of heavy fighting ensued, which resulted in the Japanese invaders being forced back to the beach on which they landed. They were then evacuated by landing craft. This was the first time in the war that a Japanese force had been unsuccessful in its mission.

At this time it would seem that the Australians were capable of defending the island. They had turned back the Japanese threat from the landings at Buna, which had resulted in an enemy force moving across the Owen Stanleys to approach Port Moresby from the west; these attackers had been driven back to their beach and farther. The latest threat at Milne Bay had been repulsed and thrown back into the sea. Further, it was at about this time that the stunning Allied victory had occurred at the battle of the Coral Sea. Though the Allies lost the carrier *Lexington,* it had not been sunk by Japanese action, but had been blown up by an explosion caused by the ignition of gasoline fumes which, during the rush of combat, had accumulated below the landing deck and had not been dispersed. The triumph of the Allied navy was that the Japanese were turned away from their intended invasion of Port Moresby and were effectively denied the opportunity to resupply the landing at Buna. This sealed the fate of the invasion of the north coast of New Guinea.

As it was decided at Allied Headquarters by MacArthur, if the Japanese were to be thrown into the sea from the Buna beach, then troops must be found to accomplish this task. Though the Australians had, at Milne Bay, done just that, there were thought to be too many invaders at Buna (Intelligence — G-2 — estimated there to be a battalion) for the Australian division (the 7th) to tend to and continue to look out for the remainder of the island.

In a training camp near Rockhampton (north of Brisbane in Queensland, Australia) was the American 32nd Infantry (Red Arrow) Division commanded by Major General Edwin F. Harding. Harding had been a West Point classmate of Robert L. Eichelberger, who as a major general, was also coming to the area to assume command of the U.S. I Corps, which at the time was the senior U.S. ground unit fighting the Japanese. The 32nd was a National Guard unit from Michigan and Wisconsin that, while having a bright record in World War I, had not yet seen combat in World War II. When it had been decided by MacArthur to retake New Guinea, the 32nd, which had first trained in temperate climate combat near Adelaide, was moved to a camp near Brisbane to gain experience in tropical combat and was again moved some 300 miles farther north to the Rockhampton camp.

The use of terrain and the logistics for the New Guinea reinforcement and the elimination of the Buna enclave proved a challenge. The sea out of which the Japanese had come was very shallow and could not have been used for the Japanese landing had it been opposed, as opposition would have entailed a fire support retaliation necessitating deep draft cruisers and destroyers. And the Allies simply couldn't stand off the beach at Buna and pound hell out of the Japanese until they were annihilated. To reach them, it would be necessary that the Allies take the same route that the Japanese had taken to the southwest, or come along the coast from the east after crossing the Owen Stanleys east of Port Moresby. The third approach was to come along the coast from the south and east (Milne Bay), though this maneuver and the resulting landings would require special boats of shallow draft with suitable capacity for troops and equipment and sufficient power and range to get loads of troops to target in reasonable time.

Because the troops that would reinforce the Australians were in Australia, it would be necessary to bring them by expeditious means to New Guinea, shuffle them around a bit, and then take them to the battle. Time being of the essence, it was decided to airlift troops to New Guinea, with some elements coming by fast sea movement. The troops traveled as light as possible because, once they arrived at New Guinea, they would still be quite a distance from the site of combat, which could not be reached by most vehicles.

From the 32nd Division, two regimental combat teams were formed: the 126th Infantry Combat Team and the 128th Infantry Combat Team. Each was comprised of a regiment of infantry, a platoon of the 114th Engineer (Combat) Battalion (Engr.(C) Bn.), a medical collecting company and medical clearing platoon of the 107th Medical Battalion, a portable 25-bed hospital, and a detachment of the 32nd Signal Company. A few jeeps and an airborne dozer were included, but interestingly, the 81-mm mortars, though they could be carried by hand, were left behind, as were all the weapons of the cannon company. And so the Japanese were to be dislodged by riflemen supported by light and heavy machine guns, 60-mm mortars, and faith in their own ability to rout the Japanese.

After the hard-won struggle to retake New Guinea, MacArthur let it be known that there were sufficient Australians ashore in New Guinea to defend the island against the Japanese, but more were needed to dislodge them immediately. (What is now known is why it was necessary to dislodge them immediately.) MacArthur's plan was to have the Australians hold the Japanese against the sea until American reinforcements arrived and then send the new arrivals to positions on the right flank of the Australians. In attack it was intended that the Australians head straight in along the Kokota Trail while the Americans attacked the Japanese left flank. The combat teams were sent from Australia to New Guinea by boat and plane during the latter part of September 1942. These troops began to arrive just as the Australians were striking at the exhausted Japanese, who had come from across the mountains. To get a feel of the situation, the 128th Regimental Combat Team (an RCT usually consisted of an infantry regiment augmented by artillery, engineers, tanks, and medics) took bivouac in the bush on the Goldie River to the rear of the advancing Australians, while the 126th RCT went into bivouac near Port Moresby. Meanwhile, a 32nd Division patrol went looking for a trail over the mountains that would put the division in a position to attack the enemy's left flank. The situation, which had for some days seemed uncertain, then took a more favorable outlook for the Allies. Of particular note was the fact that the Japanese had not attempted to reinforce the Buna defenders, which caused Allied G-2 to conclude that they first intended to whip the Americans at Guadalcanal and then deal with the New Guinea conquest. Though the Allies never believed that the Japanese would be successful in their mission, it was good to know that until Guadalcanal had been dealt with, there would be no help for the entrenched Japanese troops.

As the situation seemed to brighten for the Allies, it was thought worthwhile to try to place the 32nd Division into their right flank position as soon as possible and, perhaps, even cut off the retreating Japanese so that they could not even access their forces on the beach at Buna. But movement following decision does not always occur immediately, and it was mid-October before the Air Forces began to ferry the 126th to a recently improved airstrip at Wanigela Mission, 65 miles from Buna on Collingwood Bay. The 128th was not so lucky, for it took them five long and tortuous weeks to walk over the Owen Stanleys and reach Soputa on November 20. The 126th, having reached Wanigela, moved closer to the conflict, this time by small motor launches that ferried the troops to Pongani, just 20 miles from the Japanese. Meanwhile, the 128th (minus the 2nd Battalion, left behind to tend to other assignments to come) had been airlifted to the new strip from their bivouac in Soputa. Unfortunately, the "bush wireless" had alerted the Japanese to the reinforcement of Allied troops by the addition of the 32nd Division. This was learned by the intelligence gained by Australian patrols while probing the Japanese lines. Surprise had been lost.

The American and Australian forces began to advance on the enemy, who they thought to be no more than battalion strength and easily subdued. There had even been some mention that the Japanese, once realizing the futility of attempting resupply, would surrender or could be contained and forced to a quick capitulation.

The advance found the Australian 7th Division moving northeast toward Sanananda Point along the only improved road in their sector and using a bush trail to advance on the village of Gona. The American 32nd Division was advancing north along bush roads — better than trails, but not as good as improved roads. The 1st Battalion of the 128th Infantry was on the coast road moving toward Buna, while the remainder of the regiment was in and around Dobodura/Ango/Simeni. The 126th Infantry was somewhat in the rear around Inonda. The engineers were busily engaged in building an airstrip so that resupply could be done by air. Reports from Papuans gave the encouraging news that the Japanese had retreated to Buna, giving rise to speculation that it would all be over shortly.

The actual battlefield on which the forces fought was no more than four miles by one mile in plan dimension. The Buna mission (a group of three government houses and a dozen native shacks) was at the north of the defense position, while Cape Endaiadere was at the south. An enemy defense line surrounded Sanananda Point, and before the point position, several miles southwest along the paved road, were prepared battalion strong points.

The rivers that course down the north slopes of the Owen Stanleys meet the northern swamps that lie inland from the coastal land. These swamps, consisting of mangrove, sago, and nipa trees, are so flat and so permeable that the rivers become lost, not to reappear until the rising coastal land begins. The land area before the defensive position and lying northeast of Ango Corner, Ango, and Simeni was virtually impenetrable due to the closely spaced trees and jungle vegetation. Furthermore, the land of this area is perpetually waterlogged. The drier land, of which there is less than flooded swamp, was covered with the tenacious and dangerous kunai grass that is ten feet in height, thick, and has leaves that are about the dimensions of a pencil and are sharp enough to cut flesh if one tries to penetrate a thicket. So thick was this area that rear-line communication circumvented the area of the swamp.

The airfield that lay southeast of the mission became the most sought prize of the campaign, though it is not certain why. In Japanese hands it was of value as land but not as a means for resupply, for the U.S. Army Air Forces had virtually assured that no Japanese planes could enter eastern New Guinea territory. But as the Air Forces denied the Japanese resupply, so did terrain make formidable the American and Australian resupply, and likewise their approach to the Japanese from the sea. Coral reefs lie immediately offshore and extend for a distance of 20 miles to sea. Anything that comes ashore must do so in a New Guinean double canoe, which is limited to no more than a ton of cargo. Roads are equally challenging. Those not "improved," as was the only road that ran into the Australian position, were merely jungle paths, barely jeep width, meandering to encompass both drained high ground and frequently flooded low land. Streams were crossed by foot bridges, some of which, like that on the Girua River, were destroyed early by the retreating Japanese and required repair by the combat engineers before the road could be restored to continuing traffic. Throughout the campaign area, the engineers were constantly improving road conditions by corduroying the roads. The one platoon of engineers for each infantry regiment was kept busy.

The weather at the time of the battles was, typical of the jungle, uncomfortable. Temperatures ranged from a nighttime low of 70 degrees to a daytime high of 90 degrees, which was exacerbated by the constant humidity of 80 percent and the frequent daytime rains that measured 15 inches per month. Malaria and dengue were a near-certainty for every American and Australian soldier that served in the campaign. Though there are no statistics for the Japanese, it is surmised that their toll was as great. Quinine and Atabrine only suppressed the symptoms of malaria. There were no such miracle drugs for the results of dengue fever, typhus, and dysentery. At the height of the fighting, for every two battle casualties, there were five from sickness.

Major General Tomitaro Horii, Commander of the South Seas detachment of the Japanese army, had drowned while attempting to cross the Kumusi River during the retreat from the attack on Port Moresby. He was succeeded by Major General Kensaku Oda. Other units than those listed in the Japanese order of battle were the 73rd Anti-Aircraft Artillery, the 55th Field Artillery Battery of mountain guns, the remnant of the 144th Infantry, and the 14th and 15th Construction Units. The total forces available to the Japanese were about 2,300, of which less than 2,000 were frontline combat troops.

In selecting Buna and Sanananda as defense positions, the Japanese had chosen locations that could, if sea opportunities permitted, be resupplied from the water — though the shallow sea was beset with coral reefs and not easily negotiable even under the best of conditions. The defenders also knew that their location would be their last, for they could not retreat into the sea. Nor had they the inclination to surrender once bested by an enemy. Their response to location, circumstance, and position was to construct a system of mutually supporting bunkers, situated in depth on the relatively featureless terrain. The 32nd Division was the first American unit to encounter such defense, and the experience and knowledge that they gained in New Guinea proved invaluable to the jungle fights that were to follow with the Japanese.

The bunkers, which were a major feature of the Japanese defense, were formed by first digging a shallow perimeter trench, some one to two feet into the ground. Into the trench were placed standing oil drums and short (slightly taller than the drums) logs from coconut trees. The drums were then filled with sand. A sill from a long coconut log was used to cap the wall posts. In this way, each wall of the bunker was built. Thereupon coconut logs were placed to span to the opposite wall. Atop the roof, logs were placed — smaller-diameter logs at right angles to the main roof beams. Sand was placed on top of the final course of logs and also as fill around the periphery of the structure. Completed, the bunkers stood no more than eight feet above the surrounding area, and after several weeks, the exposed surface was covered with jungle vegetation, making the bunker virtually unrecognizable. Entrance was away from any attacker, and as the bunkers were mutually supporting, the entrances could be covered by friendly fire. A firing slit was at front.

In conducting a defense from such a system, the Japanese lived, at rest, in the bunkers but defended from foxholes located outside. The bunkers were so strong that they could withstand all punishment but a direct hit from an artillery shell, and this with a delayed action fuse. Snipers, firing from trees, were effective in protecting riflemen in their foxholes and also the bunkers. The trees and grassy ground cover gave a damping or reverberating effect to sound, so that it was very difficult to tell by the sound where a bullet had been fired from. Even if a bunker or a foxhole was captured and its defenders killed, it could not be abandoned by the attackers, for if it were, the Japanese would reoccupy it and make it necessary to fight for it a second time.

So dense was the foliage and so immediate the regenerative power of grass to grow that detection of enemy fortifications by eye observation was nearly impossible. The only way for the Allies to discover a Japanese position was to creep through the bush until they literally crawled upon it. Often, this was too late to anticipate the burst of machine-gun or rifle fire or the grenade that greeted intruders. Once discovered, an enemy position could be taken only from the flank, where attack was unanticipated.

Of course, air-ground cooperation, so successful on other fronts where the enemy and friendly troops could be seen, was severely limited. At first enemy positions were subject to intense air harassment prior to an attack by the infantry, who for reasons of safety stayed far away until the Air Forces had done its duty. Only then would they attack. However, the Japanese soon learned of the strategy of the Allies, and they countered by pulling their infantry back into the protected bunkers until the bombing and strafing was done. Then the Japanese defenders would return to their foxholes and, unscathed by the air strike, defend with vigor. It was not until the infantry took to advancing along with the air strike that the Japanese had to choose between staying in their foxholes and facing the U.S. Air Forces or the Royal Australian Air Force, or retreating to their secure bunkers and risk getting caught when they tried to return to their foxholes. It was in front of Buna that the need for the "yet to be" flamethrower and bangalore torpedo (a metal pipe filled with explosives) was born. Because it was the wet season, the tenacious grass that hid the Japanese defenders could not be set afire and burned away, yet it would have been amenable to searing by a flamethrower, and a tube of explosives could have been pushed forward and exploded over a foxhole without exposing the sapper.

Due to the paucity of roads, vehicles were not used, and thus supplies that reached the Allied frontline infantry came by hauling them up by hand or by airdrop from C-47s. But, the latter often mistook the colored panels laid out on the ground for a drop zone, and matériel was dropped either too soon or too late. Either way, supplies not dropped in the very close vicinity were not useful, for they could not be gotten to due to the density of the ground cover that made ground movement nearly impossible. And often supplies dropped right on target were damaged in the landing and could not be used. It became a war in which the Japanese defenders left their bunkers early in the morning, spent the day in a foxhole firing, and returned to the bunker in the night, while the attackers crawled into position in the moments before light came, jumped up to charge, secured a protected place if successful, and retreated into the grass if unsuccessful. At nightfall, the attackers returned to more secure rearward locations to await the next day and a renewed attack. It just happened that the bivouac of the defenders (their bunkers) was more attractive than the bivouac of the attackers (their bush camp out of earshot of listening riflemen of the enemy).

The evacuation of wounded became an especially vexing problem. A rifleman usually fell where he was struck, and this was often right in front of an enemy foxhole. The only way to protect the stretcher bearers who would come for the wounded was to neutralize enemy fire, if only temporarily.

On November 16, 1942, Major General Edwin F. Harding, Commanding General of the 32nd Division, accompanied a patrol of the 1st Battalion of the 128th Infantry as it moved along the road from Hariko to Boreo. It was engaged by Japanese attack and was required to defend itself in order to survive. The patrol leader, a captain, mentioned "gallantry in action" in the citation he wrote for General Harding. Harding was awarded the Silver Star.

With the 1st Battalion of the 128th at Boreo and the 3rd Battalion of the 128th at Simeni, the division had begun its major attack on the early morning of November 16. They were both going forward on the road in their sector and continued, unmolested, until they were met by rifle and automatic weapon fire just as they reached a position about 500 yards south of the New Strip at Cape Endaiadere. The rifle and automatic weapon fire could not be located so as to bring counterfire on the enemy positions, but it was clear that the Allies were under observation, for whenever they showed themselves, either to try to advance or to retreat, they were met by murderous Japanese fire. All night they waited in their positions and at daybreak tried again. For 26 long days this routine was repeated until December 14 when Buna village was taken. On December 20, the 1st Battalion of the 126th arrived at the front and took its place in the line between the 1st Battalion of the 128th and the sea. Upon the arrival of this new reinforcement, the division launched an attack on December 21, preceded by intense air strikes, which inflicted more casualties on the troops of the 3rd Battalion of the 128th than on the enemy. This miscalculation by the Air Forces did little to bolster the morale of the infantry unit. The strike made little progress against well-entrenched riflemen supported by automatic weapons and mortars. The attackers withdrew to their original positions soon after dusk.

Meanwhile, on the same day and across the great swamp, the 2nd Battalion of the 128th had moved to relieve the 1st Battalion of the 126th, which was going across the mountain to join the Australians for their attack. The newly arrived 2nd Battalion attacked up the trail to Buna Village. The attackers followed the trail until the lead noncommissioned officer, Sergeant Irving Hall, F Company, spotted a threatening Japanese machine gun and diverted the advancing troops before the machine gun could fire. The troops were saved, but the attack had been stalled. The infantry simply could not make any headway on the trail in the swamp grass and bush. Where they first encountered the Japanese defenders, the defensive line extended outward, and this came to be known as the Triangle. It was there on the 21st (and day after day later) that some of the bloodiest fighting of the campaign took place.

General Harding, the nominal Commander of American forces (being the senior one on the ground), organized his forces to accomplish best the tasks that had been given to him by Generals Eichelberger and MacArthur — namely to drive the Japanese from the island. On November 22, when the 2nd Battalion of the 126th was released by the Australians (to whom it had been attached), it moved up the Ango road to support the 2nd Battalion of the 128th. These units (and their front) became known as the Urbana Force/Front. The great swamp lay on the right flank of the zone of operations of this force, commanded by Colonel James W. Mott (Commander of the 126th Infantry and, on New Guinea, the 126th RCT). East of the swamp the 1st and 3rd Battalions of the 128th and the 1st Battalion of the 126th comprised the Warren Force/Front, first under the command of Brigadier General Nanford MacNider. After MacNider was wounded the day after he assumed command, Colonel Tracy Hale, Jr. (Commander of the 128th Infantry and the 128th RCT), took command of the force and the front. The command structure was taking on the semblance of a crazy quilt, even though the great swamp stood between the two forces and virtually eliminated sorting out the units and their Commanders, so that battalions of a regiment would fight side-by-side rather than attached to a foreign force or a part of a combat team made up of a conglomerate of units. The situation foreboded that if victory were not immediately forthcoming, trouble might arise as units became separated due to terrain features. But it was not until New Year's Day of 1943 that the command was again reunited. Until then, each force fought as if there were no other war in the world. This was, indeed, reality. For lodged as they were on an island and separated from their closest allies by the great swamp, there was truly nothing in the world but themselves.

Immediately after forming the new command structure, General Harding ordered attack. On November 24, Urbana Force began attacking the Triangle. Units of the 128th struck the nose of the Triangle and swung around the east to strike that side, while 126th units struck the west side. The advance of the right flank units of the attack had easy going for a time until they passed the relatively open ground southeast of the salient; then they were pinned down by the murderous fire of the Japanese in entrenched positions. If they were to retreat to safety, they would have to leave behind their 60-mm mortars and light machine guns. The forces on both sides of the attack retreated and broke off the engagement. The attack had proved that the enemy was located in very secure entrenchments. Thereafter, attacks would be directed elsewhere.

On Thanksgiving Day, November 26, the Warren Force broke into action with a strong attack toward the sea and through the Duropa Plantation. The attack was made on a front of about a thousand yards and extended from the new airstrip to the coast. This time it was hoped that artillery would be of some benefit to the attackers. With this hope, General Albert Waldron, the division artillery officer, had managed to get a battery of his own 105-mm howitzers (Battery A of the 129th Field Artillery), two troops of Australian 25-pounders (the 1st and 5th Companies of the 2nd Regiment of Field Artillery), and one battery of mountain howitzers (3.7-inch) into position and began a pre-attack bombardment. It was later discovered that this had merely cut down a great number of palm trees, which made the advance more difficult, but had inflicted no casualties on the Japanese. In conjunction with the artillery pounding, the Air Forces lent their support. From dawn, for an hour, P-40s strafed the enemy positions. Then for half an hour, A-20s bombed the area thoroughly. When the infantry jumped off and waded into the Japanese positions, they were met by machine guns, snipers, and even some mortar fire. At nightfall, the foot soldiers were no farther than at the beginning of the attack.

The results of the attacks had been so dismal that the division called a three-day deferment so that the situation could be evaluated and new plans made. On November 30, the attack resumed on the Urbana Front and made some limited headway when Company F of the 128th cut Japanese communication between Buna and Sanananda when it took Siwori Village, halfway between them. Company E of the regiment reached the outskirts of Buna Village but failed to take the grove halfway between the village and the apex of the Triangle.

The attack by the Warren Force was also launched on the 30th. It was led by Company A of the 128th, which almost immediately encountered a log barricade protected by several machine guns. Unable to get close enough to silence the guns, the attackers brought up a 37-mm anti-tank gun in an attempt to tear the barricade down. But the spongy coconut trunks, of which the barricade was made, simply absorbed the armor-piercing projectiles. No high explosive rounds were found, as they were in scarce supply.

In front of the Warren effort, there was a little salient pushed out ahead of the fortified Japanese line that, just like the Triangle to the west, came to be synonymous with trying, failing, frustrating, wounding, and dying. It appears on the maps as just north of the eastern end of the New Strip. From this strongly fortified location, the Japanese defenders could fire into the Duropa Plantation and down the axis of the strip. Supporting machine guns assured protection for others who were charged by American infantry. On the western end of the New Strip (at Simeni Creek), the Japanese were discovered to have built a similar defense system that controlled the Old Strip and secured the western part of the defense line at the

Duropa Plantation. Again and again in the first and second days of the attack, the infantry tried to force both of the strong points, each time with costly casualties. Air support had proven of no value, and the Navy could not get close enough to help. Artillery, while able to keep Japanese heads down, had to be lifted when the U.S. Infantry advanced. And when the artillery fire was lifted, so were the heads of the Japanese defenders, who then began their incessant fire on the Americans. Clearly, the effort so far by the Americans was not successful, and something new had to be tried.

On December 1, Lieutenant General Robert L. Eichelberger, Commander of I Corps, arrived in New Guinea at Dobodura. That evening, in Port Moresby, he met with the theater Commander, General Douglas MacArthur. According to Eichelberger's historians, Jay Luvaas and John Shottal, MacArthur believed that casualties were slight in the attacks then underway, which meant that the ground Commander, General Harding of the 32nd Division, was not aggressive enough to get the job done. Eichelberger recalled later that MacArthur said to him in effect, "Bob, I'm putting you in command at Buna. Relieve Harding and anyone below him who won't fight. If it is needed, put noncommissioned officers in charge of the units below the battalion. Whatever is necessary, do it. AND DO IT NOW! I WANT YOU TO TAKE BUNA OR NOT COME BACK ALIVE!"

The day after his arrival, Eichelberger visited the fronts and saw the seeming impossibility of the missions that had been given the units and also the hopeless state of confusion that prevailed. The mixed units — battalions of different regiments, fighting side-by-side with an alien Commander — could not function as they had been trained to do, and there was no help in their dilemma as long as Harding, the Division Commander, chose to fight units as he did.

The relief of Harding was no easy matter for Eichelberger — at least so he has written. Though he had not interacted with Harding since the West Point days, he nonetheless felt some comradeship and compassion for him, at least via the "West Point Protective Association," as Army Reserve and National Guard Officers despairingly referred to the proclivity of Academy graduates to protect each other. But he had been ordered to get rid of Harding, and all his subordinate Commanders as well.

Two days after being given the assignment, Eichelberger fired Harding and sent him home, along with his two aides and his Silver Star, for which the citation reads "For Gallantry in Action" — all the reward that Harding took with him when he left New Guinea. His chief of artillery, Brigadier General Albert W. Waldron, took over the division. Eichelberger, as Commander of the newly arrived I Corps, merged his Headquarters with that of the 32nd Division, and thereafter it was called the Buna Force Headquarters. Colonel Clarence A. Martin took command of the Warren Force and Colonel John E. Grose the Urbana Force. Not content with this upheaval, Eichelberger reached down even to battalion level and replaced most of the Commanders there as well. No activity was permitted on the fronts for several days while the Commanders and soldiers came to know each other. Supply was reorganized, and soon equally distributed amounts of ammunition (and in the proper size), food, and clothing began to appear at company supply dumps. Occasionally, the infantry could expect a hot meal. Quietly, so as not to arouse Japanese suspicion, units were pulled out of the line and replaced with other units, so that after a month the units of a company were returned to their parent company, and battalions were in their own regimental sector. The mess had been sorted out.

On December 5, Bren-gun carriers — small, full-tracked, open-topped cross-country vehicles, somewhat like a small tank, which could carry personnel — were brought into the conflict for the first time. They attacked the Japanese positions in the Duropa Plantation and, at first, because of the element of surprise, they moved deeply into the grove of coconut trees. As soon as the Japanese sensed what was happening and discerned the nature of this new foe, they countered by sending snipers into the trees, which they could climb with ease while under fire. From the elevated vantage, they were able to pick off the crews of the gun carriers, for the vehicles had open tops. Once disabled, soldiers on the ground could get close enough to the vehicles to kill the crew with hand grenades. The vehicles were soon deserted, as the infantry advance retreated, leaving only the abandoned vehicles and the dead. By evening, the Japanese had stripped the vehicles of their weapons.

The Urbana Front was active. Buna Village was the objective. Eichelberger, Waldron, and two aides went to witness the attack, and Eichelberger's aide and Waldron were wounded by snipers. But by nightfall, the Americans had pushed through to the sea. The village was endangered for the first time. The Warren Front rested from the incessant attacks of the preceding days. A new American line had been formed, due to the modest successes of the attacks. It ran from the sea east of Buna Village around the coconut grove, and west of the Triangle to the Ango trail, where the great swamp was encountered. Past the swamp the line picked up again, paralleled the strip, and ran through the plantation to the sea.

On the Warren Front, Brigadier General George F. Wooten, Commanding General of the front, received another rifle battalion and seven U.S. light tanks. In a spirited attack, the Australians and the tanks broke through Duropa Plantation and reached the sea at Cape Endaiadere. Another wedge had been driven. On December 19, the 1st and 3rd Battalions of the 128th crossed the bridge at Simeni Creek and, together with the 1st Battalion of the 126th, took the New Strip. The Old Strip followed as a prize to these attacks. By December 29, the enemy had been driven back to the Government Plantation. Buna Village fell on December 14th to the 3rd Battalion of the 127th Infantry, and the coconut grove soon followed. But the Triangle held against repeated attacks from December 17th to the 20th. Finally, after repeated attacks, the Buna Mission fell on January 2, and all organized resistance ceased on the Urbana Front. This ended the bitter struggle for New Guinea.

The American units engaged in the New Guinea campaign numbered 13,645 entering battle. Casualties included 800 killed, 2,200 wounded, and 8,000 incapacitated because of sickness. The casualties were disproportionate to the prize. The Japanese, having been driven back over the Owen Stanleys, could have been contained for the duration of the war by a well-supplied force of 800 men — the number that was killed to take the positions. There was no chance that the Japanese could have resupplied the garrison; the sea was too shallow and the risk of the United States Navy too great. The engagement was an ego trip for MacArthur. After this show, he learned to temper his desires in order to seek the enemy, test his strength, and, if it was found to be such that victory through attack would be too costly, simply bypass the stronghold and starve it into submission. Never again, not at Guadalcanal nor Iwo Jima nor anywhere else in the Pacific, would such casualties be taken for such a trifling prize. Luckily for MacArthur, there was not an oversight agency as part of the military to review the conduct of Commanders to judge if casualties were worth the gain. If there had been such, MacArthur would have never made it to the war's end.

Chapter 3

Fredendall's Lack
of Preparation

*L**LOYD R. FREDENDALL** was the son of a New Yorker who had traveled to Wyoming to make a new home. The elder Fredendall became active in Western politics and was an officer of the Quartermaster Corps during the Spanish-American War. After the war, he remained in the Army.*

Fredendall was born in Wyoming before his father went to war. Young Lloyd subsequently decided upon the Army as a career, and his mother, influential and persistent, obtained an appointment for him to the U.S. Military Academy from Wyoming Senator Joseph Warren. But Fredendall fared poorly at the Academy and was dismissed in 1902 because of academic mathematics deficiency. Undaunted, his mother persuaded the Senator to reappoint her son. The reappointed Fredendall lasted but a year and instead matriculated at the Massachusetts Institute of Technology, from whence he took the examination for an Army commission in 1906. He placed first among 70 applicants and became a second lieutenant, U.S. Infantry, in 1907.

Fredendall served in France during 1917-1919 in a division, on several staffs, and as commandant of an officers' training school. He ended the war with the rank of lieutenant colonel.

In 1923, he graduated high in his class at the Command and General Staff School at Fort Leavenworth, Kansas. His appointment to the Inspector General's Department in 1934 signaled that he was marked as one who would go high and far.

In 1935, as he left the IG Department, he became a colonel. Three years later, he was a brigadier general and less than a year later a major general, commanding the 4th Infantry Division at Fort Benning, Georgia — the Army's first completely motorized division. He was judged an excellent trainer of soldiers and in less than six months was in command of II Corps Headquarters in Delaware. He commanded this corps in the North Carolina maneuvers of 1941 and later that year commanded the XI Corps headquartered in Chicago. Marked as being one of the shining stars, Fredendall was selected to command the II Corps in the African campaign.

Though Dwight D. Eisenhower was critical of Fredendall's mistrust of the British Allies, he nevertheless put him in for his third star — lieutenant general. But trouble came at Kasserine Pass, where Fredendall was relieved. He returned to America to receive a promotion to a three-star general and command of the 3rd Army (training) in Memphis, Tennessee. He received a disability retirement in 1946 with the rank of lieutenant general.

Since the fall of France in June 1940, the Mediterranean had been a German lake. Whenever the Allies ventured in, such as to supply the Malta

Major General Lloyd Fredendall, who was relieved of command of the U.S. II Corps at Kasserine because he threatened to uncover the flank of his French ally. Despite his relief, he was later promoted to lieutenant general and headed a stateside training army. (U.S. Army Signal Corps)

garrison (which they attempted several times during 1940-1943), it was at their peril. It was far better to take the long route around the Cape of Good Hope at the southern tip of Africa than to endure the endless harassment of the German Luftwaffe. But this route added 10,000 miles, and supplies and time were critical. If the Allies could secure North Africa from Axis occupation (where Field Marshal Erwin Rommel was) and from the occupation of those who favored the Axis (all of the Vichy French possessions of North Africa), then food and supplies that came to Germany from Africa would come to a halt. The control of French North Africa would assure that Suez and points east would be safe from German threat, that Dakar in the Senegal would no longer be a haven from which Germans could harass Atlantic shipping, and that a possible springboard to invade Europe would be taken. In addition, the reestablishment of friendly relations with the French could be achieved if the repossession of French African colonies could be done without angering France.

All this and more was at stake, and thus the Allied planners at the head-of-state level believed the schemes that had been proposed to them to be possible and of the next priority. Consequently, in the summer of 1942, General Dwight D. Eisenhower was instructed to begin planning for his move, which proved to be a bold one — to control all of North Africa.

Upon the fall of France, Admiral Jean François Darlan, head of French naval forces, had caused the majority of the French fleet to secure itself in safe harbors in French North Africa. There it remained, lethal and waiting for whoever might gain its favor. The Allies were determined to try to win over the French warships, or at least put them out of action so that they would not be used against possible Allied moves.

Eisenhower and his planners saw a multiple strategy and multiple and simultaneous landings as the best way to accomplish their desired results. It was decided to divide the striking force into three parts: the first (western) striking at Atlantic possessions — Morocco; Casablanca, and Fedala (now Mohamadia), Port Lyautey (north of Rabat), and Safi (south of Casablanca); the second at Oran; and the third at Algiers. The first group would secure the French warships, as were found, and try to make contact with the second, which after taking Oran would strike both east and west, attempting to make contact with the landings on either flank. The Algiers landing was to hold to the west, but strike boldly to the east with the ultimate task of capturing Tunis and Bizerte. Spain had let it be known that it did not intend to interfere in the effort as long as Spanish neutrality was not challenged by an Allied incursion into Spanish Morocco, which lay between Oran and Casablanca. However, Eisenhower had to contend with the possibility that an enraged Hitler (realizing that Spain would take no part in the North African caper) would retaliate by invading Spain and

Left and opposite page: From *U.S. Army in World War I: Mediterranean Theater of Operations, Northwest Africa: Seizing the Initiative,* by George F. Howe (Washington, D.C.: Dept. of the Army, Office of the Chief of Military History, 1957), 18-19.

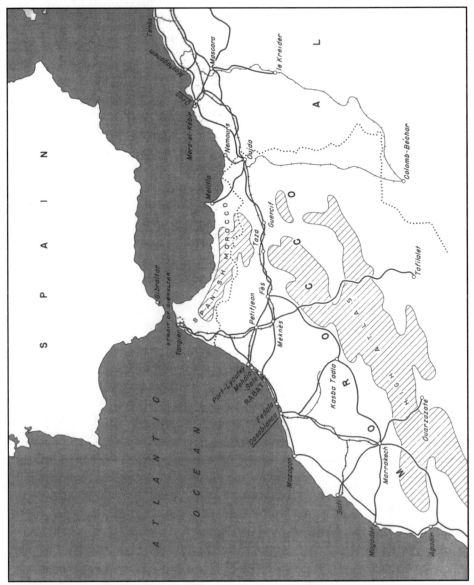

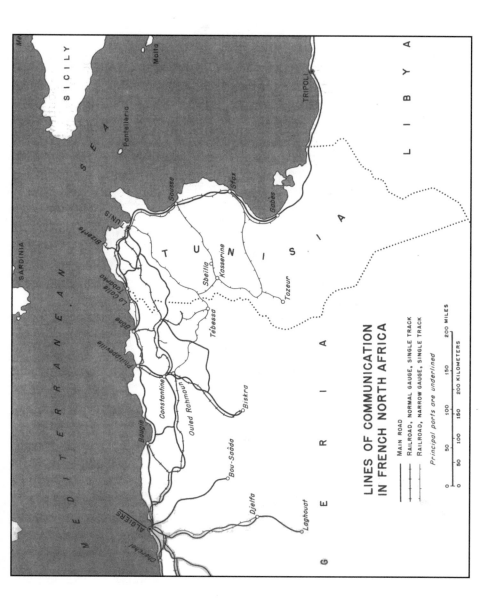

LINES OF COMMUNICATION
IN FRENCH NORTH AFRICA

MAIN ROAD
RAILROAD, NORMAL GAUGE, SINGLE TRACK
RAILROAD, NARROW GAUGE, SINGLE TRACK

Principal ports are underlined

0   50   100   150   200 MILES

0   50   100   150   200 KILOMETERS

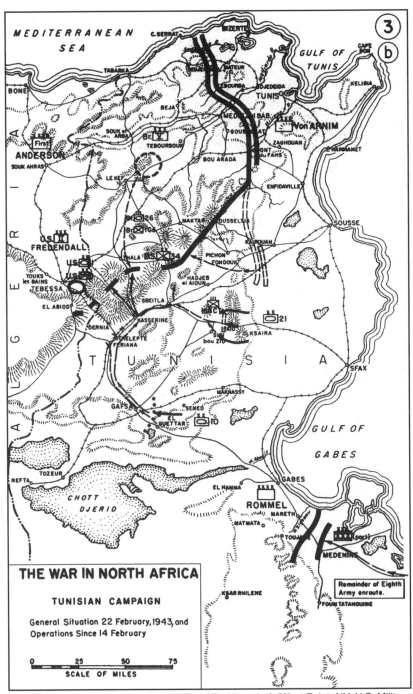

From *The War in North Africa*, Part 2 (*The Allied Invasion*) (West Point, NY: U.S. Military Academy 1944)

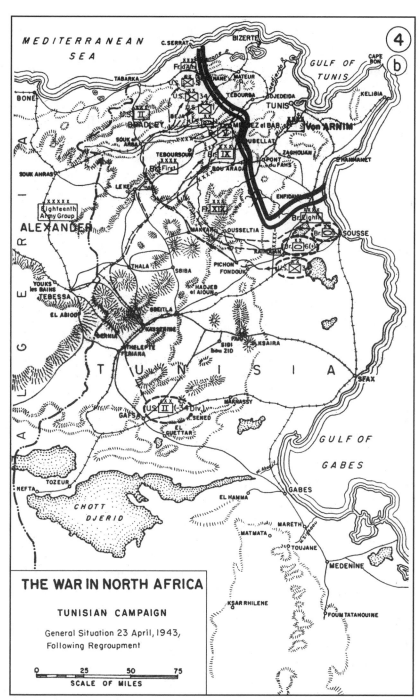

From *The War in North Africa*, Part 2 (*The Allied Invasion*) (West Point, NY: U.S. Military Academy 1944)

overrunning Gibraltar. If this happened, it could be overcome or corrected in the long run. But during the North African invasion, it would have proven most difficult to resupply into the Mediterranean if Gibraltar was held by Hitler.

While French officers commanded forces in Africa, most of the soldiers were Moroccans, Senegalese, Tunisians, and Algerians. It was not at all certain how the loyalties of these troops would lie. French crews on the warships were also an uncertainty, but it had been decided to go in and try to persuade the French not to resist. Should resistance occur, the Allies were prepared to do battle with the French and best them. Early in November, Eisenhower and his staff were flown to Gibraltar to be close at hand to direct the invasions.

The Allies used visible deception and strategies to confuse the German navy's observers. They stood off Dakar to cause the Germans to believe that it was there they would strike rather than Casablanca. The convoy taking the invasion to Oran and Algiers took on speed and gave the impression that it was racing to resupply Malta when it passed the straits of Gibraltar. The Luftwaffe refrained from bombing the ships, but from its lair in southern Italy, France, and Sicily, it awaited the crucial moment when it would pounce on them with the combined strength of planes in the Mediterranean. That moment never came, for after steaming past Oran and then past Algiers and then even farther, the fleet suddenly turned south and at forced speed made for the points where it was to disembark troops to invade. The landings took place on November 8, 1942.

The battleship *Massachusetts*, aircraft carrier *Ranger*, and a cruiser squadron headed by the *Brooklyn* began landing the 3rd Infantry Division and the 2nd Armored Division at 5:00 a.m. at Casablanca, some two hours after the other two landings at Oran and Algiers. The surf was greater than had been anticipated, and landings were difficult. French warships (the battleship *Jean Bart*, the cruiser *Primaguet*, and destroyers that had been in harbor) made for the open sea to challenge the invasion. The French ships opened fire on the Americans, and they returned it. Soon the *Primaguet* and two destroyers were hurt and were beached to prevent their sinking. There was little damage to the *Jean Bart*.

During the previous night, Admiral Darlan, who headed French forces in Africa, had come on radio and told French forces to cooperate with the Allies and to offer no resistance. The instructions were heeded at Casablanca; however, at Port Lyautey, Safi, and Fedala, there was naval resistance and strong firing from shore batteries. Later, in the early stages following the invasion, on December 24, 1942, Admiral Darlan would be assassinated. A serious credibility gap might have occurred had not General Henri Giraud made his escape from occupied France and, after a voyage aboard an Allied submarine, arrived in North Africa to join the cause.

At Port Lyautey, the American battleship *Texas* and the cruiser *Savannah*, together with screening destroyers, made the initial invasion approach that November 8th. When French searchlights were turned on them, French shells began to fall, and the heavy ships had to move out of range of French guns and send the attacking force ashore by a longer route.

By the end of the first day, all intended landing parties on the western sites were ashore and moving to secure their initial and secondary goals. General Ernest N. Harmon, who commanded the Safi force ashore, soon gained his objective and moved to join the force in Casablanca, which he found had capitulated to the Americans. Only the cease fire, arranged by Giraud, stopped the fighting between the French and Americans at Port Lyautey. The regimental combat team of the 9th Division and the landing team of the 2nd Armored Division, commanded by then Brigadier General Lucien Truscott, were having to plow through heavy seas and were surely grateful for the decision of the French to lay down their arms. With this, the action in the Atlantic ended. The ocean was secure from Nazis.

Elsewhere, much was being done other than just fighting. Some time after his success in persuading a tempered and successful occupation of Morocco and before he fell to the assassin's bullet, Admiral Darlan had told the French fleet in Toulon, in southeastern France, to put to sea and join the Allies and French troops in Tunisia to resist the Germans, who were yet to arrive, and to help the Allies before and when they arrived. Hard on the heels of the Allied landings in Tunis and Oran, the Germans immediately set to invade Tunisia. When they did they were not opposed by the French military, though they had been so ordered by Darlan.

In Algiers, the American Navy began to attempt to put troops ashore in the early dawn of November 7, but they were met with stern resistance. On a second attempt, an American destroyer broke through the boom that protected the harbor and raced for the dockside to disembark the landing force. The fire returned was so intense that it was decided to retreat from the harbor and await the completion of landings being made both north and south of the harbor. Fortunately, these landings were successful and began to converge on the central location. The harbor force was put in again, and all three forces converged, linking up in the late afternoon.

In Oran, on the same day, it was much the same as in Algiers, but French resistance to the Americans was stronger. An attempt to force the boom and penetrate the harbor failed, but the landings to the north and south were successfully lodged on land and slowly began to make progress to unite. In the afternoon, the airfield had been captured. The next day, slow but steady progress was made, and the units joined. Here, too, the local resistance ended, and this had all been accomplished without the need to use the paratroops who had been held in readiness.

The first phase of the African operation had ended, and two Allied forces were poised — one in the east under British Field Marshal Sir Bernard Montgomery, who just then had the Germans on the run and was about to enter Tripoli, and the newly established force on Africa's west coast and in Oran and Algiers, commanded by Major General Fredendall.

The order Darlan had issued for French forces to join the Allies in resisting Germans was, as expected, countermanded by the pro-Vichy forces in Tunisia. The consequences of this resistance were not to the liking of the Allies. The Germans were virtually invited in, and they responded by airlifting 1,000 to 1,500 combat troops into the country every day. Soon their forces were becoming formidable, and those who were part of the recently successful landings at Tunis and Algiers were told to turn east and make all haste to be the first to reach the peninsula at the Gulf of Tunis. It was at this time that the Americans who were moving to the east were organized into the II American Army Corps under the command of Major General Fredendall. At this juncture in the campaign, a person of the boldness of Erwin Rommel, General George Patton, or Civil War Generals Jeb Stuart, Phil Sheridan, or Nathan Bedford Forrest was needed — one who could think and who would "get there the firstest with the mostest." But German Colonel General Hans-Jürgen von Arnim was the Commander who seized the peninsula and the cities of Bizerte and Tunis and who would cause the Allies quite a bit of trouble before he was done.

To reach Tunis from Algiers, as the Allies had to do, necessitated traveling 380 miles; to reach Tunis from Tripoli, as von Arnim had to do, necessitated traveling 460 miles. Armored Commanders and mechanized cavalrymen, such as von Arnim's force, are generally faster and more bold than foot troops; this may explain why the Americans, principally foot soldiers, arrived last with the least. When they were 50 miles west of Tunis, they encountered German patrols. Rather than test whether or not they were confronted with a meeting engagement (two military forces, each moving toward the other and meeting, neither having assumed a defensive position), they hunkered down and began to dig in and await further orders from above. Actually, had the Americans done but a bit of probing, they would have discovered that the Germans occupying Tunis were few in number and the majority of their forces were yet occupying what were believed to be strategic places along the route from Tripoli — each of these places being one that Rommel thought would possibly be struck by the Allies. Little did he know, at the time he began his move to Tunis, that it would be he, not they, who would deliver the first blow. While there were numerous skirmishes along the way between the Germans and the Americans on the west, at Algeria, and the British on the south and east, there was yet to be a prolonged stand. Rommel's retreat from Tripoli to Tunis could be likened to that of Confederate General Joseph E. Johnston retreating to Atlanta before Federal General William T. Sherman in 1864 — it was skillful and conserved his forces, but to what purpose?

The Americans were more easily held off than the British. On the Maknassey-Senid-El Guettar Line, the Germans were holding. But when threatened by the British 8th Army, advancing from the south, they retreated northward. On April 7, the two armies — the British 8th and the German Afrika Korps — met between Gabes and El Guettar. By strokes of good tactical direction, Field Marshal Montgomery had captured more than 20,000 of the enemy since the offensive had begun on March 21, though these losses were by no means devastating to Rommel. With von Arnim holding west of Tunis, Rommel had to choose a defensive line from which he could reasonably expect to be resupplied from Germany and eventually break out. On the north, Sedjenane was the most appropriate commanding ground from which to have the flank protection of the sea. Next, to the south, was the village of Medjez el Bab, which was on the rail line into Tunis and lay between two commanding ridges. Farther south was Pont du Fahs, and after that there was not a clear choice. Should he refuse the line to Enfidaville (a defensive position that has been bent around or at right angles at its end so that the end is protected from the rear by the defensive soldiers facing rearward), bringing the whole of the Afrika Korps into the enclave of the Gulf of Tunis, or leave a flank dangling by extending southwest to include the commanding ground at Kasserine?

Rommel thought it would be wise to defend this latter ground, where it would be possible to have a springboard from which to launch an attack that could drive the Allies back to the sea and cut off much of the American strength.

By early April, a cohesive and defined front between the British and the Germans had developed. Lieutenant General Kenneth Anderson's British 1st Army was on the north, with the British IX Corps on its left flank. Adjacent to them was the XIX French Corps, and on its right was the II American Corps under Major General Lloyd Fredendall. They were to hold the right flank position of the 1st Army and maintain it until they could be joined by Montgomery. Rommel knew, of course, that of his adversaries, the Americans were the least battle-tested, and his grand plan — to strike north, reach the coast, set confusion to reign, and gain the initiative — was furthered in that he would face American forces who were just then digging in at the heights, which included a terrain feature known as Kasserine Pass.

Eisenhower, in Gibraltar, was aware of the concentration of adversaries at the Tunis Peninsula and could envision theater Commander Field Marshal Sir Harold Alexander's and Montgomery's plans (to entrap von Arnim and Rommel) and Rommel's plans (to cut Alexander off from Montgomery and defeat them singly). He paid a visit to the site of the impending battle on February 13 and found that the II Corps had dug itself into a "deep and almost inaccessible ravine a few miles east of Tebessa," quite a way from the battle front. At the II Corps Headquarters, Eisenhower heard the din of hammers and drills and learned that the corps engineers were tunneling into the sides of the ravine "to provide safe quarters for the staff." Eisenhower, in *Crusade in Europe*, states that he "quietly asked" if these engineers had already assisted in preparing defenses at the front, but a staff officer, "apparently astonished at my ignorance," indicated that the divisions' own engineers would do that. Eisenhower notes: "It was the only time, during the war, that I ever saw a divisional or higher headquarters so concerned over its own safety that it dug itself underground shelters."

Eisenhower then began an all-night inspection of the front lines and discovered "a number of things that were disturbing": first, the complacency of the II Corps, which then was made up of the 1st Armored Division and 1st Infantry Division, along with the 34th Division. (The 9th Division was supposed to join up as well.) The corps had delayed — inexcusably — to perfect its defense positions in the passes. And this, said General Eisenhower, was due to the Commanders' "lack of training and experience." Mine fields had not yet been planted, with the excuse that the infantry had just been in the area two days — but that the corps would begin the next day to put out the mines.

One can only imagine Eisenhower's amazement at this casual response in a battle zone. He states in *Crusade in Europe*:

> Our experience in North Tunisia had been that the enemy was able to prepare a strong defensive position ready to resist counter-attack (attack?) within two hours after his arrival on the spot. The enemy's invariable practice . . . was to plant his mines instantly. . . .

But even Commanders who had been in the theater for three months had not heeded these tactical lessons, and Eisenhower "gave orders for immediate correction."

Eisenhower states that he spent the rest of an "exhausting night" with Commanders, itemizing the matters he wanted to take up with General Fredendall. But upon his arrival at Corps Headquarters, he found that the Germans had already begun their attack.

Perhaps the most glaring shortcoming of the II Corps, not mentioned by Eisenhower, was that Fredendall had chosen to occupy the ravine northwest of Kasserine but failed to occupy the high ground to either flank — a grievous error.

The attack by von Arnim began on the morning of February 14 and seemed to be directed toward Kasserine. Eisenhower's G-2 (Intelligence) believed this to be a feint, but, in fact, the main attack was yet to come and would be directed toward Fondouk. When Eisenhower learned of this on his return to Allied Forces Headquarters, he promptly fired the G-2. Great captains, though they plead for tolerance to be shown to themselves, rarely show it to others.

Montgomery's 8th Army tried to come to the aid of the Americans, but they were held up at a defensive position south of Gabes with the gulf to the northeast and the mountains at Toujane to the west — both terrain barriers. Rommel felt that he could hold off the 8th until he dealt with Alexander. He was to be surprised, however, for on the night of March 23-24, Montgomery sent the New Zealand Corps and Army Reserve around the mountains to the west and two days later surprised the Italian defenders of El Hamma/Matmata. Realizing that his forces were in danger of being divided, Rommel abandoned the Mareth Line — a German defense line running from the mountains on the south to the gulf on the north, passing through the village of Mareth and located at the base of the peninsula of Tunisia. But this all came after the II Corps had itself been dealt a pounding at Kasserine.

The defensive position that Fredendall had chosen, before the pass at Kasserine, featured rather abruptly formed mountains standing before the gently sloping plain that stretched away to the coast. The terrain was treeless, save some small scattered scrub trees. Other desert shrubs were infrequent, and the ground was without grass. The prominences were mostly without trees and were exposed rocky surfaces. As Eisenhower had found, Fredendall had chosen to defend the valleys, and his defense lines stretched from mountain to mountain. This decision was probably influenced by the roads that penetrated the mountains and led to Tebessa and Thala, both to the north. They were hard surface (blacktop) and, though narrow in width, were adequate for military tracked vehicles in the attack.

In choosing to defend the valleys, Fredendall (and certainly his Division Commanders) ignored the possibility that the enemy could infiltrate up uncovered wadis — gullies — in front of the mountains and ascend the mountains undetected. From there they could look upon the American defenders in the valley below them. The main interest of the Germans was in the American anti-tank guns and their crews, for Rommel had planned an armored attack up the roads and needed to silence the opposition.

At the time of the battle, the Americans' principal infantry weapon against tanks was the 37-mm gun, which came from the pack-mounted, wooden-wheeled gun of World War I. The French 75-mm piece was being used by the artillery as an indirect-fire machine and was not considered for direct fire. Meanwhile, Germany, who knew what others would use to combat their tanks, simply built tanks with such armor that the guns set against them were ineffective. The British had learned the hard way that their small-size anti-tank guns were ineffective and had upgraded to a new 57-mm gun, which had a much higher muzzle velocity and a more suitable armor-piercing projectile.

When the Germans struck on February 14, 1943, they quickly downed the outposts, which retreated to main lines. The German patrols then began to make their way up the wadis and thence up the mountains. When in place, they began to fire on the defenders below, with most of their targets being the anti-tankers. As anti-tank potential was neutralized, Rommel struck with his tanks. There was nothing in the American arsenal to counter them, and the Germans could move, unimpeded, through the infantry. All that the Americans had to stop German armor was American armor, and it was necessary to get deep into the American lines before this armor was encountered by the Germans.

For the armored attack, von Arnim relinquished his Chief of Staff, General Heintz Ziegler, so that Ziegler might lead a corps attack comprised of two Panzer divisions. Rommel personally led the German left (flank): the Centauro Division and the active German portion of the Afrika Korps. To the left of the U.S. II Corps was the XIX French Corps under General Alphonse Juin.

The 21st Panzer Division had tried and failed to penetrate the French lines at Sbiba Pass, but they were successful, led by Ziegler, on the front before Kasserine. There, also on the 20th, the 10th Panzer Division and the Afrika Korps broke through the road leading up to the pass, thrusting onward. Once penetrated, the II Corps lines moved right and left against the terrain protection that was given by the mountains. Fredendall informed Juin, on his left, of the penetration and told Juin that it appeared he, Fredendall, would have to choose between fighting to retain either Thala or Tebessa. He did not have the resources to do both. Fredendall opted to defend Thala and abandon Tebessa.

Juin was furious, and for several reasons. First, he believed that had Fredendall mined his front, as Juin had, the German tank attack could not have penetrated so far into American lines. Juin blamed Fredendall for allowing enemy patrols to gain the mountaintops and neutralize the crews of anti-tank guns. Finally, and most telling, Juin could point to the criticality of Tebessa. It was his lifeline of supply, and if it were lost, he would have no route of resupply nor of retreat should the Americans, by their retreat, allow the French position to be flanked. There were acrimonious words between the two, and though in the end Fredendall agreed to try to hold Tebessa, the argument of the day had been enough for Juin to report the incident to General Anderson, Commander of the 1st British Army in which both the French and the American Corps were serving.

Anderson saw trouble between the two and asked Alexander, Commander of the Army group, what should be done. Alexander called Eisenhow-

Looking northeast from the village of Tebessa at Kasserine Pass. (U.S. Army Signal Corps)

American infantry advancing to the Kasserine Pass. (U.S. Army Signal Corps)

er, who was in Gibraltar trying to find reinforcements to help stem the tide that was running against the Allies. When Eisenhower found out that Fredendall had proposed abandoning Tebessa, he remembered how Fredendall had dug himself into the mountains while mines had yet to be laid. Apparently, Fredendall had harbored the idea of pulling back and allowing Germans to flank Juin.

The situation between Juin and Anderson was quite interesting. When the French had come into the picture, they insisted on operating independently of British command and only under Eisenhower's generalized leadership. To achieve Allied harmony, Eisenhower had agreed to do this. Now he was confronted with a case in which the French were appealing to the British — Juin to Anderson.

Eisenhower was herein confronted by a conundrum. At the very moment that Alexander and Juin were urging that something should be done about Fredendall, there was before the United States Senate the nomination of Lloyd Fredendall to be a lieutenant general in the Army. It had been put before the Senate by Eisenhower himself, albeit with the approval of General George C. Marshall. If Eisenhower were to relieve Fredendall from command of the II Corps, what was he to say about the glowing words that he had already uttered in support of the promotion? Most of the Corps Commanders of World War II were major generals, and only those few who were long tried and found not wanting were promoted to lieutenant general. But it was not characteristic of Eisenhower to admit that he was wrong or that one of his decisions need be overhauled. In *Crusade in Europe,* he wrote that after the first of March he replaced Fredendall with Patton as Commander of II Corps.

> I had no intention of recommending Fredendall for reduction or of placing the blame for the initial defeats in the Kasserine battle on his shoulders, and so informed him.

Eisenhower states that he and others shared the responsibility for the "week of reverses." However, the morale of the II Corps had been jeopardized, and Eisenhower thought that General Patton was just the person to solve the problem. He stated that he believed Fredendall was "better suited" for a training position stateside than he was for battle, and he recommended to General Marshall that "Fredendall be given command of an Army in the United States, where he became a Lieutenant General."

Fredendall left the II Corps on March 3, George Patton took his place, and Fredendall returned to America to become the Commander of the Mid-Continent Zone of the Interior Army, a post that he held until war's end. During that time, the middle of America was not attacked by a hostile power, and thus history did not have the opportunity to see the talent of Lloyd Fredendall in commanding a field army. But one might say that he was promoted in order to get rid of him.

Chapter 4

Brown's Raw Deal — Attu, the Unnecessary

*A*LBERT E. BROWN, *of Charleston, South Carolina, was born in 1889 and graduated from the U.S. Military Academy in 1912, becoming a second lieutenant, U.S. Infantry. He waited four years to become a first lieutenant. His first posting was the 4th Infantry at Fort Crook, Nebraska, from where he went to Galveston, Texas, in 1913. The next year he went to Vera Cruz, New Mexico, for six months' duty, then returned to Galveston*

Major General Albert E. Brown, 7th (Hourglass) Division, was relieved by the U.S. Navy in the Aleutian struggle just as he reached victory, because he had put the battleship *Pennsylvania* in danger. (U.S. Signal Corps/Library of Congress)

with the 4th, which was moved to Brownsville, Texas, and then Gettysburg, Pennsylvania.

In the fall of 1917, he joined the 59th Infantry at Camp Greene, North Carolina, and in May 1918, he sailed for France. He served as adjutant of the 8th Brigade for several months and then became adjutant of the 183rd Brigade in the St. Die sector-Vosges Mountains, where he participated in the Meuse-Argonne offensive. Following the Armistice, he served with the 92nd Division, returning to America in 1919.

After brief assignments he became an inspector for the 8th District, Reserve Officer Training Corps, at Kansas City, Kansas. From 1919 to 1923, he was professor of military science and tactics at the University of North Dakota. In 1923, he attended the Infantry School at Fort Benning, Georgia, and the Command and General Staff School at Fort Leavenworth, Kansas, from which he graduated in 1925.

Following a tour with the 11th Infantry in Indiana, he spent three years on staff duty in Hawaii and then attended the U.S. Army War College at Carlisle Barracks, Pennsylvania. He graduated from the Navy War College in 1931. He spent four years on the War Department General Staff in Washington and then became a member of the Infantry Board at Fort Benning, where he served until 1938 when he commanded a battalion of the 38th Infantry at Fort Sill, Oklahoma. During 1940-1941, he served on the General Staff of the War Department in Washington, having been promoted to brigadier general in 1941. He was sent to the 7th Infantry Division, Fort Ord, California, and in May 1942 became its Commander as a major general. After a short (classified) assignment outside the U.S. he returned to command the Infantry Replacement Training Center, Camp Wheeler, Georgia. He was the Commander of the 7th Infantry Division in the Aleutian operation, and after being relieved by the U.S. Navy, he traveled to the European theater for duty with the 35th Infantry Division to command the Ground Force Reinforcement Command. At war's end, Brown was Commanding General of the 5th Infantry Division. He brought this division back to America and, at Camp Campbell, Kentucky, retired a major general.

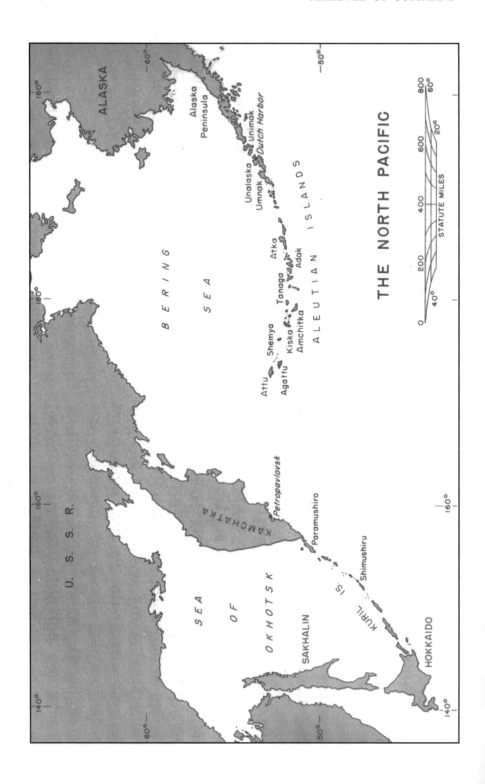

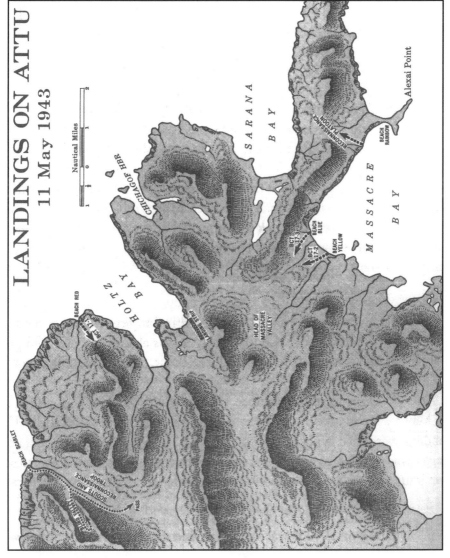

LANDINGS ON ATTU
11 May 1943

Nautical Miles

The Aleutian Islands extend as a gentle arc 1,000 miles from the southwestern mainland of Alaska toward Siberia — a chain of varying dimensions and size inhabited by Aleut who give their time to fishing and hunting seals and other creatures. The islands are the last place on earth that one would expect a hostile power to challenge the sovereignty of the United States. What would there be to gain from acquiring any of them?

For most days and nights of the year, the islands are fog-shrouded or experience the constant and continued drizzle of the Pacific Northwest or the howling wind of the open sea of the North Pacific. Their harbors are poor and the tidal flow exceeds 20 feet. Their terrain countenance is mostly exposed rock with scant soil available for civilization to flourish. Today, in the face of global exploitation and a population explosion, the islands remain much as they were 50 years ago when the Japanese chose to take them.

It is now thought by some terrain and strategic thinkers that Japan perceived, incorrectly, that a toehold on one or several of the islands would be a stepping stone to Alaska and thence to the mainland of North America. Whatever the Japanese planners thought, little did they reckon with the bleakness of what they had bought, or with the inexplicable ire that they had created in America, which motivated action disproportionate to the significance of the prize soon to be fought over.

Had America been wise, she would have simply contained the occupation of the islands taken by Japan so that through harassment and interdiction of supply, the Japanese presence would have become more of a joke than a threat. The Allies did, in fact, follow a similar course of action in the aftermath and exploitation phase of the OPERATION OVERLORD landing on the coast of France in 1944. The Allied front advanced into the continent and moved toward Germany. German forces, isolated against the sea on the right flank of the advance, retreated onto the peninsula at Brest. There they met an Allied push to take the port of Brest. The Germans demolished the port and retreated onto the narrow spit of land north of the port. There they occupied no more than 400 square miles of France and posed no threat to the Allies. The defenders could be observed constantly by land, sea, and air. They simply could do no mischief. Brest fell on September 19, 1944, and the defenders fell back onto the headland. As the harbor was in shambles, the Allies made no attempt to use it. Allied planners are thought to have concluded that the remaining pockets of German occupation were not worth the life of one Allied soldier in the taking. Consequently, they were left unencumbered, but contained, until the war's end. The German defenders and the Allied containers at St. Nazaire even struck up some modicum of friendship while shelling and sniping at each other along the 20-mile front.

But the Aleutians were different. They were America, and their occupation by Japan remained a bone in America's throat. Thus, it was ordered that they be retaken. Given the tenacity of the Japanese at the moment, it would be by the force of arms.

If there be, in more recent military and naval history, a counterpart to the taking and retaking of the Aleutian Islands, it would be the 1982 conflict over the Falkland Islands in the Atlantic, off the coast of Argentina. As in this brilliant accomplishment by the British, the retaking of the Aleutians was done simply to assuage the pride of the country. The two achievements established, in a small way in the North Pacific and a large way in the South Atlantic, that there are some things that simply must be done and for no other reason.

To the historian, the Japanese activity in the Aleutian Islands was part of the grand scheme of Admiral Isoroku Yamamota. This scheme was to culminate in a naval victory in the Coral Sea, followed by a victory at Midway, followed by the occupation of the two outermost islands of the Aleutian chain, Attu and Siska. But after the naval engagements at both the Coral Sea and Midway, in which the Japanese achieved far less than they had hoped, the Americans claimed victory in both.

Subsequent to these naval battles, the Japanese occupied the two Aleutian Islands. It has been surmised that the landing and occupation of the two undefended islands occurred on June 6-7, 1942, begun on the last day of the Midway engagement. It was carried out by a task force under the command of Vice Admiral Hosagaya Bishiro. Three infantry battalions of the division commanded by Major General Juichiro Mineki, which came from Hokkai, made up the occupying force and set about fortifying the positions as if to defend rather than to use them as a stepping stone to other conquests. Because no major airfields were attempted to be built, it is surmised that perhaps the Japanese simply wished to deny the Americans possession of the islands, possibly to forestall their use from which to launch some kind of attack on the Japanese homeland. Soon the Japanese began to call the troops on the islands the Hokkai Garrison, giving it a further air of permanency, at least in Japanese eyes. Despite heavy harassment by the Americans, a resupply of the Hokkai Garrison was completed on October 24, 1942, accomplished by the merchantmen's carrier and destroyers escort.

Before the landings on the two islands, the Japanese had bombed Dutch Harbor on Unalaska several times in early June 1942, though little damage was done to American military installations as a result of these bombings. However, on one of these bombing runs, on June 3, several Zero fighter escorts did battle with a slow-moving American reconnaissance plane. An American machine-gunner on the reconnaissance plane hit one of the fighters, which landed, disabled but virtually intact, on American soil at Akutan Island. It was immediately recognized that this was a great prize of war. The plane was disassembled and transported back to the production plant of an American aircraft manufacturer. It was studied in detail, and a retaliatory counterpart, the Grumman F6F Hellcat, was designed by the American engineers. The new American fighter aircraft came into production in just 18 months, and it did much to win the war in the Pacific.

A week had transpired before American reconnaissance planes discovered that the Japanese had occupied two of the Aleutian Islands. The turmoil that ensued in America was akin to that which followed the Japanese bombing of Pearl Harbor. The American response to the occupation was to reinforce heavily the American forces defending Alaska.

Major General Simon Bolivar Buckner, Commander of the Alaskan Defense Command, urged immediate reprisal for this threat to his domain. His superior, Lieutenant General John DeWitt, heading the Western Defense Command, concurred, as did Rear Admiral Robert Theobald, naval Commander of the North Pacific under Admiral Chester Nimitz. General George C. Marshall deferred immediate action, being fearful of the effects of the abominable weather around the islands. But with Marshall's approval, plans were drawn and forces selected to land troops and retake the islands, Attu first and then Kiska. Meanwhile, the Americans could only bomb the two Japanese positions (when weather permitted) and try, by naval forces, to prevent their resupply.

Admiral Theobald began to assemble the forces that he could get to begin the retaking of the islands. General Buckner, whose forces continued most of the bombing attempts, fumed at what he perceived as the Navy's lack of aggressiveness. On most of the bombing runs, the islands were obscured by fog and clouds and were not visible from the air. Bombardiers struck by "departure time from points of reconning" and hoped that some of the armament found the Japanese or their installations.

The 7th U.S. Infantry (Hourglass) Division, which had long been stationed in warm and benign Hawaii, was selected as the ground force that would be landed, first on Attu, then Kiska. It is hardly possible to find a more abrupt and traumatic change in climate and environmental conditions than from Hawaii to the Aleutians. The division, commanded by Major General Albert E. Brown, was well disciplined and as well trained as could be expected of a division that had never seen ground combat. The troops had participated in stateside maneuvers, both woodland and desert, but these experiences would do them little good in the Aleutians, which had no trees for concealment nor sand in which to dig for cover.

Planners in the War Department and on down the quartermaster chain began to consider the clothing needs of the 7th Division in the northern climate, and ordnance officers fretted over the functioning of arms and vehicles. Slowly, re-equipment supplies began to arrive in Hawaii, and they were quickly issued to troops who tried to envision how cold and miserable it would have to be before the heavy uniforms would be comfortable.

Under Rear Admiral Charles H. McMorris, who commanded his battle units and attack force, Admiral Thomas Kincaid immediately established a naval blockade of the waters leading to the occupied islands. Meanwhile, Vice Admiral Hosagaya needed to be able to repeat the replenishment operation that had been done on October 24, 1942. To do this he sent two cruisers (*Maya* and *Nachi*) with destroyers to escort two fast merchantmen laden with supplies. On the picket line were the U.S. cruisers *Richmond* (light) and *Salt Lake City* (heavy). The two forces met as the Japanese approached Attu. The *Salt Lake City* scored several hits on the *Nachi* in a long-range duel of naval gunners, but the cruisers did manage to decoy the Americans away from their quarry, the merchant ships loaded with supplies. The *Salt Lake City*, old and firing at odd and uncomfortable angles, damaged herself during the firefight. As a result, she was incapacitated in steering and was only able to turn with great difficulty. American destroyers laid a smoke screen so that she could hide, but she was nevertheless hit by one of the Japanese cruisers. This blow, together with damage-control confusion, rendered her dead in the water. Sensing that the Japanese would turn and shell the *Salt Lake City* to the bottom, McMorris ordered his destroyers to the suicidal task of torpedo runs on the Japanese cruisers. The

American destroyers steamed toward the Japanese despite salvo after salvo that fell around them. But before the American destroyers had reached a position from which to launch their torpedoes, Hosagaya broke off the engagement and steamed away home. In spite of his anguished reasoning that he had retreated because he was running low on fuel and ammunition and he was expecting an immediate American air attack, he was relieved of command on his return home and assigned to a naval reserve command. The sea battle of the Komandorski Islands, as it was called, produced the first casualty of command — Admiral Hosagaya. There was to be yet another.

It is now known that the Japanese forces numbered three battalions, about 1,800 men, plus the supporting troops, which raised the total to more than 2,300. The Americans wisely sent a combat division plus supporting troops, amounting to more than 16,000; they thus outnumbered the Japanese seven to one.

The map of the theater shows that the mountain slopes on Attu to the south and east are more precipitous than those from the north and west. The mountains are treeless and tundraless, with steep rocky slopes. The valleys are flat and covered with low, matted tundra, which impedes walking or vehicular movement but offers little concealment and no cover. The almost inaccessible Sarana Bay lies just north of the easternmost extremity of the island. The limited data from aerial reconnaissance and dubious data from the observation of previous visitors led to the conclusion that Sarana Bay was inaccessible to seaward landings and to contact from elsewhere on the island; it was thought that there were no Japanese entrenched there. Both Massacre Bay on the south of the island and Holtz Bay on the north had flat, gentle beaches. The harbors were deep water, allowing landing craft to approach, and the harbors seemed to lead to somewhere. They were chosen for the main American landings, though on the north it was intended to place troops ashore in the valley west of Holtz Bay.

Though the American invasion was to have taken place on May 7, 1943, the nemesis of the campaign, weather, prevented the landings until May 11. Landings took place at five Attu beaches (see table opposite page).

The invasion forces were assembled at Cold Bay on Adak in the Andreanof Islands. On May 11, surf, tide, and visibility conditions were for the first time all favorable for the landings. In positioning themselves,

Location	Troops	Mission
1) Beach Scarlet	Divisional "scouts" and partially dismantled reconnaissance troops	Sweep to Holtz Bay
2) Beach Red	Regimental Combat Team 17-1	Secure Holtz Bay and link up with troops from the south
3) Beach Rainbow	Reconnaissance troops	Move north to Sarana Bay and secure flank (?) of main thrust
4) Beach Blue	Regimental Combat Team 17-2	Secure Massacre Valley, link with 17-1, find Japanese defenders and defeat them
5) Beach Yellow	Regimental Combat Team 17-3	

however, two of the landing craft — the vessels *Sincard* and *MacDonough* — collided and were lost to the action.

It has been surmised that Japanese intelligence had realized that America was about to attempt to regain the occupied Aleutian Islands. Several contradictory, but nonetheless enlightening, bits of information pertain to this short moment before the battle. A Japanese convoy bringing troops to Attu was turned back because of an awareness that Americans might get there at or about the same time. Several destroyers, thought to be possibly an evacuation force to remove occupying troops from Attu, turned away during the beginning of the invasion. The few Japanese vessels in Attu, several landing-type craft thought to be of little value in prior supply operations, would have been of insufficient capacity to handle the Japanese troops in an evacuation and were of no use to oppose the landing of the enemy.

Major General Albert E. Brown, commanding the U.S. Army's 7th Infantry Division, had planned to land Regimental Combat Team (RCT) 17-1 at either Beach Red or Beach Scarlet, depending on which of the two was judged to be the more favorable, based on the report of scouting reconnaissance parties to be put ashore prior to the landing. Their primary role would be to link up with the other two combat teams. The roles of those landing at the other northern beaches would be to secure Holtz Bay and assist in the linkup with the two other RCTs.

All of these preparations and plans were based on the assumption that the majority of Japanese defenders found on the island would be those at Chichagof Harbor and at the high ground separating Holtz and Massacre Bays. It was also speculated that the ridge between Massacre and Sarana Bays would be defended, although, as this was an extended terrain feature (it was a ridge three miles in length), it would be only lightly defended. It was also believed that once in place, defenders would have no other place to go and would remain at their posts until surrender or, much more likely, death.

At Beach Scarlet, the scouts were first landed with the intention that the reconnaissance unit would follow once the foot soldiers had reported that the way was clear for vehicles — light cavalry. The scouts trudged toward the south and in the early afternoon reached a pass, some three miles from their point of landing. Supplies were dropped to them there. They reported no enemy soldiers encountered. The movement of wheeled vehicles was impossible south of the pass.

RCT-1 went ashore at Beach Red in early afternoon. The beach area was easily secured, but enemy gunfire from the Chichagof area was stirred up, and thereafter a brisk exchange continued. Troops were landed throughout the remainder of the day and on into the night. The beach was secured, and on the next day the troops would move south.

Massacre Bay was different. The troops that put ashore at Beach Blue had become oriented to the northeast instead of the northwest and were confronted with the precipitous rock face of the ridge arising from the sea. When reporting their dilemma, they were instructed by Division Headquarters to go along the coast to their left until the gently sloping sedimentary valley was found. Shortly they found it, and their land adventure began. As the Navy soon realized that the coxswains in the landing craft were all going off to their intended left and putting troops onto the cliffs, it was decided to place the destroyers closer to shore so that the mother ship — the troop ship — could better direct the courses of their spawned landing craft. Then, as if to be especially fickle, the fog lifted and the landing proceeded, observed by the landers and unimpeded by the defenders.

By midafternoon, the three RCTs had been landed, and only then did the enemy realize that the Americans were upon them. Though the Navy had landed Army troops, the Navy believed that their role of shelling shore installations should begin even though there was no call from the Army or evidence that shore installations needed to be shelled. But shelling began by the U.S. Navy, and it was responded to by the Japanese wherever shells fell. Soon there was fire and counterfire on several fronts.

At its western termination, Holtz Bay is divided into two arms. On the morning of the 12th it experienced a bifurcated attack — troops going to one side or the other of the headland that divided the bay at its apex. Some Japanese defenders fired upon the invaders from positions in the foothills at the front of the approaches to the valleys leading away from Holtz Bay. The Army Air Forces (AAF) obliged by bombing the southernmost position and the Navy the northernmost. The *Idaho* (a battlewagon involved with the invasion) fired 14-inch shells at what might be shore positions at both locations. Throughout the afternoon of the 12th, Japanese artillery fire increased and became a serious deterrent to the advancement of the invasion. Further, the terrain and surface trafficability proved to be a great obstacle to movement. A significant number of troops became occupied with nothing more than trying to help extricate trucks and weapon carriers stuck in the mud. At the end of the day — D+1 — the situation ashore was barely better than it had been the day before. Of particular concern was the scarcity of actual combat troops, created by the need for so many helping hands to assist the mired vehicles to reach their destination with necessary supplies, ammunition, and food.

On this second day of the invasion, the Navy had a few mishaps of its own. A torpedo was fired at the battleship *Pennsylvania* offshore of Holtz Bay, but through evasive action she was able to avoid being hit. One of the transport group vessels (the *Perida*) struck a pinnacle rising from the ocean floor and began taking water in two of her compartments. She was ordered to beach herself. With the help of hydrographers, she was able to find passage through water of sufficient depth to reach the beach. Her cargo was taken by sister ships, as was her role in the landings. The aircraft carrier *Nassau*, independent of the Fleet with but one destroyer to provide submarine protection, sailed within distances offshore that varied from 10 to 40 miles. Her planes could respond more quickly than AAF planes operating from Dutch Harbor.

General Brown's troops suffered 44 men killed and more than 200 wounded on the first day. The two battalions that had begun their way up the valley at Massacre Bay were pinned down by machine-gun fire and unable to advance. Brown called for a reserve battalion (the 3rd Battalion of the 32nd Infantry) to be committed in order to strengthen the pressure on the Massacre Bay defenders.

May 13, D+2, came with fog and no promise of improvement. Beach Red had been shelled all the previous night by the Japanese and the shelling intensified with daylight, inhibiting the unloading of boats. The divisional artillery attached to the two landing forces was unable to get guns into position to begin direct fire support of the infantry. Brown had his command post on Beach Yellow and from there was trying to direct the operations of Yellow, Blue (on his right flank), Rainbow (three miles to his rear where troops were trying to reach Sarana Bay), Red (all the way across Holtz Bay where troops were trying to link up with the forces attempting to advance up from Massacre Bay), and Scarlet (to the west of Beach Red where troops were mired at the top of the pass).

The confusion and uncertainty was exacerbated when on the 13th reports began to spread that there were Japanese landings of reinforcements in Holtz Bay. Brown, disturbed by the spreading of rumor and by what he hoped was misinformation, sent his Assistant Division Commander to take charge of the other beach in the bay, Rainbow. Though he had quieted the rumors, he was fast using up his senior Commanders to gain control in Massacre Bay, all to the detriment of the other locations of a widely scattered and missioned command.

The situation in Holtz Bay was interesting. Landings were being challenged by Japanese artillery firing from barges located in the bay. So effective was the fire from these barges that artillery of RCT 17-1 had been unable to set up its own firing. But the Navy solved this problem by silencing both the artillery and automatic weapons from these barges and enabling the 17-1 artillery to get into position and begin firing, which then allowed the unloading to take place uninterrupted.

Meanwhile, Brown's call for reinforcements had been answered; a battalion of the 32nd Infantry was landed at Beach Red on the afternoon of the 13th to strengthen RCT 17-1. Late in the evening though, Brown again called for more reinforcements from those waiting in Adak. The Navy retorted that it was running low on ammunition.

A strong attack by the two RCTs in Holtz Bay on the morning of May 14 supported by the fire of a destroyer and the *Pennsylvania* allowed the troops to advance about 500 yards, but no more. General Brown was to assert, "As long as you are firing continuously, we can advance — keep it up!" But the Navy was running out of shells. By that afternoon, D+3, the battleships *Nevada* and *Idaho* had shot all their 14-inch explosive ammunition and were ordered to sail away to a haven north, safer from the increasing threat of submarine activity.

On May 15, D+4, the ships that were still unloading in Holtz Bay reported that this activity was progressing and nearly complete. Next came the question of how to get the unloaded supplies to the infantry, if they were to advance.

Again, Admiral Kincaid, the Task Force Commander, received a message from General Brown that the reinforcements he had several times requested "might make the difference between the success and failure of the operation." Brown asked that Kincaid call a conference so that all might know of the ground situation that prompted his requests. In early afternoon, Brown came aboard the *Pennsylvania*, the pennant ship, and again stated his need for reinforcements. Good news came from Holtz Bay where RCT 17-1 had advanced from the northernmost arm of the bay and had gained contact with troops from Beach Scarlet. The men there had been able to transcend the difficult terrain conditions encountered at the top of the pass. Beach Red, however, was still under heavy artillery fire from the southern arm of the bay.

May 16, D+5, was to be a fateful day for Brown. In the early hours, three sections of American fighters had strafed Holtz Bay, and two had been lost. Other planes continued air support, coming in and out of fog to do so. A B-24 Liberator was unable to use the unsecured airfield in south Holtz Bay, and thus the load of supplies was dropped on Beach Red. On the positive side, the forces from Holtz Bay and those from Massacre Bay united. With U.S. forces now combined, the Japanese retreated up the narrow pass to the east and began moving into the hills overlooking Chichagof Harbor.

Task Force Commander Kincaid was told that he was to receive a battalion of the 4th Infantry from Adak, which would arrive the evening of May 18, D+7. Kincaid then gave naval control to Captain Herbert B.

Knowles, who previously had commanded one of the transport ships. The *Pennsylvania* and the aircraft carrier *Nassau*, together with supporting ships, withdrew to the north in order to be more protected from submarine threat. Cargo ships that had discharged their loads departed for Adak.

In the late evening of the 16th, Major General Albert E. Brown was informed rather tersely by radio communication direct from Admiral Kincaid that he was relieved of command. No reason was given. Major General Eugene Landrum took his place as Commanding General of the Hourglass Division. Perhaps the captured Japanese documents that showed the enemy's strength to be 2,000 to 2,500 men — far fewer than Brown had asserted — had some bearing on the decision of the Task Force Commander to remove Brown. His removal was also likely out of concern for the safety of Navy ships from torpedo attack, particularly those that had spent all of their ammunition and were of no further use to the invasion. Whatever the reason, Brown was out and Landrum was in.

On May 17, D+6, the enemy had been driven out of the southern arm of Holtz Bay. Casualties from the cold and frostbitten feet, in particular, were the primary reasons for the lack of soldiers to man the foxholes. The day after Landrum took over from Brown, Landrum reported that though he had driven the Japanese from Holtz Bay, he, too, needed reinforcements: two rifle companies, a battery of 105-mm's, and a Headquarters unit and Commander.

For the next nine days, American forces continued to consolidate, drive the Japanese farther into the harbor area around Chichagof, and generally improve their conditions. Artillery had been brought up close into the narrow valley overlooking the harbor and was controlled by the division under the direction of the Artillery Commander, Brigadier General Archibald Arnold. Engineer and other supporting troops had come to occupy positions in the rear of the infantry and within the valley. Late on the night of May 28, the Japanese began preparation for their last great effort — to move up the valley, cut off the linkup north to south, overrun the land supplies resting on the ground at Massacre Bay, re-equip themselves, and again retreat to the hills to await the arrival of reinforcements. At dawn on the 29th, D+18, the Japanese attacked and quickly overran the position of the 3rd Battalion of the 17th Infantry. Apparently the Japanese were loose in the valley. General Arnold rallied a defensive reply and began to assemble whatever rear position troops were around. These troops took positions on the hill just south of Chichagof Harbor (which, after the occupation, came to be known as Engineer Hill after the division engineers who first were there to defend it).

The defense of this hill was stubborn and finally successful. The Japanese attacked several times, but their final assault eventually cost the lives of the entire attacking force. When the action was called complete, the renewed 3rd Battalion of the 17th Infantry began to pursue the remnants of the Japanese forces, and by the end of May 31st, D+20, the island was secure and victory was won. In the Attu campaign, 2,350 Japanese had been killed and 23 taken prisoners; America had 552 killed and 1,140 wounded.

Several thoughts emerge from this little conflict. The Japanese had previously accomplished their victories by taking the offensive and having numerical superiority (in Malaysia, almost two to one). In the Aleutians, however, they were on the defensive and were outnumbered seven to one. Were the Americans killing a fly with a sledgehammer? And was the sacking of Brown by Kincaid but an example of interservice rivalry? Kincaid, hardly an infantryman, knew little of what Brown was up against, and there is no record that he ever went ashore to try to learn the problems that were confronting the Hourglass Division. This was but to be the precursor of an oft-repeated lesson of the Pacific War: Whenever the officers of the U.S. Army served under a command other than their own (*i.e.*, the U.S. Navy or U.S. Marines), their commanders were in extreme danger of being relieved. It is rather interesting to note that during the same period, the Marines and the Navy lost no senior commanders to relief.

When General Brown left the Pacific area on May 16, he traveled to Hawaii and then returned to Washington for reassignment. The Army thought, privately, that he had gotten a "raw deal" from the Navy, but there was nothing that could be done about it. Brown was sent to Camp Wheeler, Georgia, to command the Infantry Replacement Training Center. After the invasion of the European continent in June 1944, he was assigned to Supreme Headquarters Allied Expeditionary Force (SHAEF) as a roving inspector and observer of frontline divisions. General Brown took command of the 4th (Red Diamond) Division on the departure of Major General S. LeRoy Irwin.

Chapter 5

Allen and Roosevelt with the Big Red One

ERRY DE LA MESA ALLEN was born at Fort Douglas, Utah, in 1888. An "Army brat" (his father was a graduate of the U.S. Military Academy in 1881), Terry Allen entered West Point in 1907, and though permitted to linger an extra year to make up a mathematics deficiency, he failed gunnery his senior year and was dismissed. Undaunted, he graduated from Catholic University in 1912 and that same year was commissioned a second lieutenant, U.S. Cavalry.

Major General Terry Allen, of the Big Red One (U.S. 1st Infantry Division), was relieved because his men liked him too much and were too boisterous in their revelry following their North African victory. (U.S. Army Signal Corps)

Allen served in the Southwest on the Mexican border through 1917, where he was in several skirmishes and rose to the rank of captain. In France, 1917-1918, he commanded a battalion of the 90th Infantry Division, was wounded three times, and gained the reputation as an aggressive leader.

On his return to America, he attended the Command and General Staff School at Fort Leavenworth, Kansas, as a major. The War College soon followed, as did the rank of lieutenant colonel. In 1940, with war clouds looming, he became a brigadier general, conveniently bypassing the rank of colonel. On his promotion, he assumed command of the 1st Infantry Division (Big Red One), which he led through North Africa and into Sicily until he ran afoul of General George S. Patton.

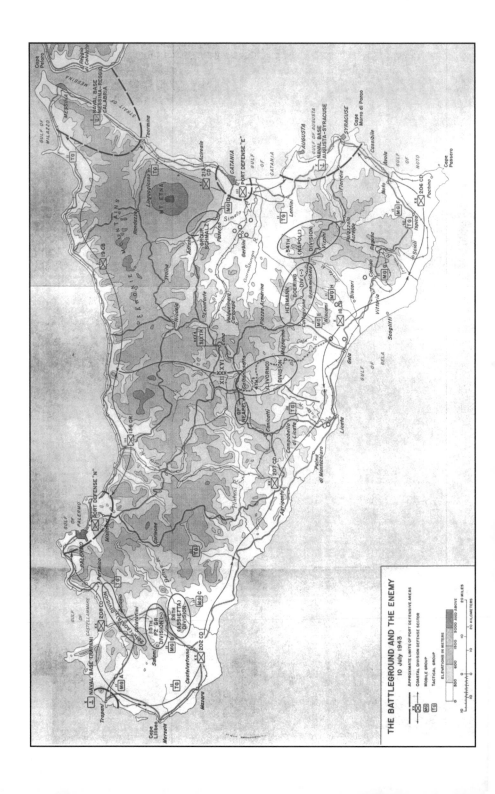

THE BATTLEGROUND AND THE ENEMY
10 July 1943

Brigadier
General
Theodore
Roosevelt, Jr.,
Assistant
Division
Commander
of the U.S.
1st Infantry
Division, was
relieved by
Omar Bradley
in the general
housecleaning
in North Africa.
(U.S. Army
Signal Corps)

In the attack on Troina, Sicily, Allen procrastinated and was
relieved. Yet "under a star," he returned to the United States
and took command of the 104th (Timberwolf) Division, which
he trained and landed in Cherbourg, France, in September
1944. After 195 days of sustained combat, he met the Russians
in Germany on April 26, 1945. He retained command of the
Timberwolves in occupation but, damaged by his iconoclastic
attitude, he never rose above his two stars, which he wore into
retirement.

Opposite: From *U.S. Army in World War II: Mediterranean Theater of Operations, Sicily and the Surrender of Italy*, by Albert N. Garland and Howard McGaw Smyth (Washington, D.C.: U.S. Army, Office of the Chief of Military History, 1965), Map II.

Theodore Roosevelt, Jr., was the son of the 26th President of the United States. Born in 1887, he received his undergraduate degree from Harvard University in 1909. At the onset of World War I, he was a major in the 26th Infantry, 1st Infantry Division, where he saw action in the battles of Cantigny and Soissons and in the Meuse-Argonne and St.-Mihiel offensives. Twice wounded, he returned to civilian life after the war. He was soon in the New York General Assembly and then became Assistant Secretary of the Navy until he resigned in 1924, in which year he was Republican candidate for Governor of New York.

He was Governor of Puerto Rico from 1929 to 1932 and Governor General of the Philippines from 1932 to 1933. In 1934 and 1935, he was chairman of the board of American Express, and from 1935 until his death, he was a vice president of Doubleday.

In 1941, he returned to active duty commanding a regiment of the 1st Infantry Division. He became Assistant Division Commander in December 1941, with the rank of brigadier general. He remained with the division in North Africa until he was relieved.

He was an observer at Normandy and died in his tent of a heart attack on July 11, 1944. He held the Distinguished Service Cross, Distinguished Service Medal, Silver Star with two Oak Leaf Clusters, Purple Heart, and numerous foreign decorations. He is buried in the military cemetery at St. Laurent, France, and received the Congressional Medal of Honor posthumously.

On October 25, 1942, the U.S. 1st Infantry Division embarked from the British Isles bound for a landing in Oran, Algeria, in what was to become the beginning of the end for the Vichy French, Mussolini, and, ultimately, Hitler. It is not known exactly how the division came to wear the red number one on their shoulders. Legend has it that the shoulder patch was fashioned from a bit of red cloth taken from a German tunic in World War I, when divisional insignia was coming of age. All the units along the western front in World War I were anxious to have identity. The 42nd Infantry — Rainbow Division — had been one of the first units to devise a shoulder patch to recognize its countrywide diversity, and thereafter, other divisions developed their own distinct shoulder patches.

No division of the American Army had a more proud heritage than the 1st Infantry. It had truly been the first divisional unit seated in the Army. Previous to its formal creation, and for years before, divisions had simply borne the name of the divisional Commander (*i.e.*, Archibald's Division). Afterward, it was decided that because Division and Corps Commanders came and went, as did Regimental Commanders, it would be wise to begin calling them by numerical identification.

In the stripped-down U.S. Army prior to the mobilization before World War II, the 1st Infantry Division was one of those that manned the thin OD ("olive drab") line and was one of the first to embark for overseas. It was commanded by the raw-boned Terry de la Mesa Allen, who, having shown himself outstanding as a leader, was promoted to brigadier general in 1941, though even at the time, the selection board had questioned his indifferent attitude to discipline. Terry thought that leadership, willingness, and the ability to fight were more the desired attributes of the soldier. When the storm clouds of the impending Second World War gathered, Allen was again promoted.

Terry's Assistant Division Commander was Theodore Roosevelt, Jr., son of the late President. The younger Roosevelt had previously served as Governor General of the Philippines and, being a reserve officer, was called to active duty when he returned from the Philippines.

In November 1942, as the 1st Division's convoy passed into the Mediterranean, the Germans mistook the intent of the movement as being for the purpose of resupplying and strengthening Malta, and the Luftwaffe decided to wait and strike after more force could be brought to bear. Deception triumphed, for after slowly steaming past Oran and being just at Algiers, the convoys suddenly turned to the starboard and raced to their destinations for the invasion. When the landings had been made and local resistance had been quieted, the Americans began a race to Tunisia and Tunis, which they just barely lost to the Germans. Hence, the American people came to know a new word — Kasserine. It was there that American anti-tank crews, badly outgunned by the German Tiger tanks, were put to humiliating defeat. The Big Red One took its lumps, too, at Kasserine,

but it left the final victory more cocky than ever, believing that it had almost achieved success alone.

When the battle for Tunis was over and German General von Arnim had
managed to extricate most of his forces unscathed, the Big Red One was
trucked back to Oran, from where it was to embark for the invasion of
Sicily. But an occurrence in the last days of the battle will allow the reader to look into the hearts and minds of the petulant little boys that were
leading thousands of Americans in a life and death struggle.

The 1st Division, which had established a command post at a small
oasis, was directing a struggle against both the Wehrmacht and the Luftwaffe, which, thinking it had little chance of gaining air superiority, gave
the Allies a good strafing whenever it found them exposed. As a result of
this, Terry Allen had directed a Standard Operation Procedure requiring
that all troops, when stopped for more than half a day, would dig slit
trenches into which they could dive if an enemy air attack occurred. Both
Terry Allen and Teddy Roosevelt dug their *own slit trenches.*

When General Patton, on his first inspection as newly appointed Commander of II Corps, visited the 1st Division command post, he found slit
trenches dug. He asked Allen where his trench was, and Allen showed
him. The story goes that Patton walked over to the trench and urinated into
it. He then turned to Allen and said, "Now, General, use that if you want
to."

One would think that such unwarranted humiliation in front of troops
would result in reprimand and even relief. But it was necessary to await
something *big*, like the slapping of the shellshocked soldier, for George
Patton to get his comeuppance — and even then hardly so. For, as in the
slapping incident, Patton thought that he was dealing with a coward in
Allen, who would deign to dig his own slit trench so that he could get into
it and *hide* when the Luftwaffe flew over. To Patton, helmet liners and
neckties and speed limits were important; what was unimportant and cow-
ardly should either be slapped or urinated on — the ultimate indignation.

When the Big Red One finished the Tunisian campaign on May 7, 1943
— relatively unscathed (though it was committed piecemeal to other
units) — it retired from the battlefield and in fits and starts made its way
back to a rest area in Oran. Having had their first taste of battle and surviving, the soldiers of the 1st Infantry Division began to loot and pillage,
wreck every bar, "beat the hell out of" every goldbricking rear echelon
soldier they found, and "go to war" with any MPs who tried to stop them.

The story is told that Terry Allen liked to recount a conversation he had with one of his riflemen during the rest period in Tunisia when the MPs were giving the celebrating men of the Big Red One a hard time and its soldiers were responding. The rifleman is alleged to have said, "General, when the war is over, I'd like for our division to come back to Tunisia and beat hell out of every goddamn MP that we could find." Such was the love that the men of the 1st Infantry Division had for discipline.

Unfortunately for the 1st, however, General Dwight Eisenhower's Headquarters got wind of the antics, by then uncontrolled by General Allen or Major General Omar Bradley, the II Corps Commander. Bradley was dressed down by General Eisenhower for the 1st Division's behavior and told to get them out of cities and into the desert and to replace distilled spirits with 3.2 beer. But there being none of the latter that side of the ocean, the 1st had to settle for Tunisian beer, which they drank from a bivouac so far into the desert that, as one who was there described it, "They had to pipe sunlight in!" By this time, it seemed to General Bradley that anyone who could cause him to be chewed out so badly had to go. He decided then and there to replace both Allen and Roosevelt, Allen because he got Bradley chewed out and Roosevelt because he probably had too many friends in high places and might cause Bradley plenty of trouble. However, there was the matter of Sicily, which was about to be fought by, among others, the 1st Infantry Division. What a nasty time to sack one who had, at Kasserine, been reasonably successful. If the sacking were to come hard on the heels of the rioting in Tunisia, the soldiers of the 1st would misinterpret it as an affront to their "old man" and, quite possibly, might give a bit of trouble in the coming Sicilian caper. Bradley thought it better to wait until he had gotten all that he could out of the 1st and Allen and Roosevelt. Then he would sack the two. And so Bradley, as is befitting all honorable and great captains, let the two condemned fight on, unaware.

Sicily, which the Allies were to invade next, is an island shaped much like a high-topped shoe, 150 miles in boot length and 100 miles in boot height. In 1942, the island was a backwater of the Italian empire suddenly thrown into prominence because of the war swirling around it. Moderate metamorphism had thrust up some of the Sicilian mountains and had created a terrain of barriers that made surface access via roads tortuous. At the time of the Allied invasion, there were perimeter roads all around the island, though many were so poor that to circumvent the island's nearly

450 miles would have required more than a week. While in some places the land rose precipitously from the sea, in most locations there existed beaches that had little more than three-foot tidal fluctuations, which were favorable to the landing of assault craft. The major roads were blacktop, but the remainder were only soil or stone-surfaced. Because little rain fell during the campaign, trafficability, where roads existed, was possible, though not ideal. But road surfaces, both improved and unimproved, soon fell to the wear of military traffic and issued forth great clouds of dust as the caravans passed.

In the defense of Sicily, the Axis Order of Battle of command and forces began with German Field Marshal Albert Kesselring, who commanded the theater. He was at the time headquartered on the mainland, shuffling between Rome and the several impending locations of action. He had as his liaison officer, attached to the Italian 6th Army, General Fridolin Rudolf von Senger und Etterlin, whose job it was to keep the Italians in line. The Italian Commander of the 6th Army was General Alfredo Guzzoni, who had been in charge but a few months, having been recalled from retirement to take the command. He had replaced the able General Mario Roatta, who had been relieved after publicly questioning whether the Sicilians had the stomach for the upcoming fight.

Under Guzzoni's 6th Army were the XII Corps, comprised of the Aosta and Assietta Divisions and the Napoli and Livorno Divisions in the XVI Corps. The 15th Panzer Grenadier Division was deployed with the 28th Aosta and 26th Assietta on the peninsula west and south of Palermo. Nearer to the heel of the shoe were the forces of the XVI Corps, comprised of the 5th Napoli and the 4th Livorno Divisions of the Italian army and the German Herman Goering Division deployed between the two to assure that they fought. Battle Group Schmalz occupied a position to the north (and rear) of the presumed location of attack. The coast was manned lightly by coastal defense units of the Italian army: the 206th Coastal Defense from Siracusa west to Ragusa, the 18th from there to Gela, the 207th met the 202nd halfway between Agrigento and Castelvetrano where the latter extended in defense past Cape Lilebeo, and the 208th completed the defense past Palermo. Guzzoni was nominally in command, and his Headquarters were in Enna.

There were different opinions among the Commanders as to how best to defend the island. Guzzoni did not believe the Axis troops could hold the island, but he did think that the best chance for success by the Italians and the Germans lay in the strategy of letting the coastal divisions take the brunt of the initial assault and then striking the landings with reserve troops. Kesselring thought the Sicilian roads to be so poor that he despaired of bringing troops into battle and preferred the strategy of meeting an attempted landing with sufficient force to throw the invaders back into the sea. Von Senger agreed with Guzzoni, and thus Kesselring compromised with a plan that wound up not as good as either. Perhaps the unmodified plans would have been more successful for the Axis.

Some of the Allied units that were to take part in the invasion were veterans of North Africa, having fought von Arnim or Rommel. When the fighting was ended in Tunis, the British returned to their base of supplies in Gabès and Tripoli and the Americans to theirs in Oran and Algiers. Among the Americans were the 1st, 3rd, and 9th Infantry Divisions. The 45th Thunderbirds of the National Guard (Oklahomans and Texans) were combat-loaded in America and transported directly to the invasion. The 34th Division remained in Tunisia in occupation, and the 1st Armored Division was busy trying to get accustomed to the new Commander, Major General Ernest Harmon, after Major General Orlando Ward. Former Commanding General Ward had been sacked by General Bradley, who didn't think it should be done — on the orders of Patton — who perhaps was too timid to do it himself — at the suggestion of Fredendall, who had himself been sacked, and General Clarence C. Benson, who had led a task force under whom Ward had served as a part of the hastily organized group!

At the Casablanca Conference between Allied leaders on January 1943, it had been decided that Sicily would be the next objective after the elimination of Axis forces from the continent of Africa. The overall Commander for the effort was to be General Sir Harold Alexander and the naval Commander was to be Admiral Sir Andrew B. Cunningham. The Commander of the British army was to be General Sir Bernard Montgomery, and the Commander of the American 7th Army was to be General George Patton. Rear Admiral Allen Kirk was to command the assault forces for the Americans; two British corps were to be used in their effort, the XXX and the XVI. The American forces were to be divided between the II Corps (commanded by General Omar Bradley) and a separate left flank unit, of Corps level, consisting of the 3rd U.S. Infantry Division and some supporting troops.

The plan for invasion called on the British and Canadians (the Canadian 1st Infantry Division was a part of the British 8th Army) to land on both sides of the peninsula southeast of the island, while the Americans were to land at beaches on the southwest — Gela, Licata, and Porto Empodecle. The British and Canadians were then to move boldly forward toward the northwest and the north coast, while the Americans, after securing the beaches, were to strike toward the north-northeast and make headway inland, taking the city of Caltanissetta. Thereupon, the plans became somewhat fuzzy, but it did seem that it was intended that the Americans and the British and Canadians, having taken their objectives, would join, and the Americans would swing left of the advancing British and Canadians and continue with them to secure the north of the island. After this was accomplished, the combined forces would swing right and pin the Axis defenders in the narrowing neck of the northeast of the island. Mt. Etna, which was thought to be a feasible strong point, would be contained by the British, taken if possible, but, if not, encircled and rendered impotent. Whatever the potential advances of either army, it was recognized that Messina, being the main jumping-off place for Axis troops to reach the mainland, was the principal objective of the campaign, for on its taking the Axis would be denied a place from which to leave the fray.

The Allied planners simply had not conceived that the paucity of roads and the pace of advance of both armies would be such as to render critical the use of the road from Siracusa to Caltanissetta. Yet, when the Americans reached the road — or were a mere thousand yards short of it — before the British had arrived, they fully believed that they would turn left and continue their attack with the British and Canadians following whenever they could. But, if the "best laid schemes of mice and men" often go awry, what about unlaid schemes? As we follow the course of the battle, we will see just such a scheme.

The first plan for the Sicilian invasion envisioned two American corps participating — the II Corps (which Bradley had only recently taken over from Patton when the latter became the Commander of the 7th Army) and the VI Corps (of Major General Ernest J. Dawley). Patton, having some doubt of the inexperienced VI Corps, persuaded Eisenhower to use only the II Corps, which he knew, and to send the VI Corps to someone else. That someone else was Lieutenant General Mark Clark and the 5th Army. (Clark took Dawley and, in Italy in September 1943, found him wanting — he failed to cover his flank. Although the result was neither disastrous nor serious, Clark canned Dawley.) And so, in proportioning the front that

Alexander allotted to the 7th Army of Patton, it came to be that there were two corps sectors on the American beaches and inland — that of the II Corps and that of the 3rd Infantry Division (acting as a corps but not really a corps). To the student of economy, the question follows: Could the effort in Sicily have been accomplished without either Bradley and the II Corps or Patton and the 7th Army?

The British navy, with its two aircraft carriers (the *Formidable* and the *Indomitable*), six battleships, nine cruisers, and 30 destroyers, provided the sea force of the invasion of Sicily. Air Chief Marshal Sir Arthur Tedder, with his strategic air group, had reduced the German airfields on Sicily to a state of uselessness, while Air Vice Marshal Arthur Coningham's tactical air arm had mastered the skies. However, American ground Commanders fretted because of lack of knowledge of what to hope or expect from the air coverers. The airborne troops might also have wondered what to expect from ground anti-aircraft. They were all soon to know.

The Sicilian campaign on the ground began officially on July 10, 1943, when British glider troops of the 1st Airbourne Division and paratroops of the U.S. 82nd Airborne Division first touched ground. But few of the glider troops made it to Sicily, and still fewer made it to the landing place. The Americans were luckier, for most of them reached Sicily, though hardly any were dropped in the American sector; most were dropped in the British sector and were spread out over 60 miles. When the paratroops of the 505th Parachute Infantry Regimental Combat Team under Major General James Gavin landed, they were so confused that they were uncertain if they were even in Sicily.

The amphibious landings were more successful. They took place in the early morning hours of July 10. The British landed four divisions and a brigade (two corps) at their appointed places, and the Americans did likewise with (starting on the left) Truscott's 3rd Infantry landing at Licata, Allen's 1st Infantry at Gela, and Major General Troy Middleton's 45th Infantry at Scoglitti. One of Allen's regiments and the 2nd Armored of Gaffey were in floating reserve.

The Americans, as well as the British, were successful in their attempts to reach their land objectives; by noon of the landing day, July 10, the 3rd and 1st were in their assigned cities — Licata and Gela — and though somewhat slowed by the surf conditions and rocky shores, the 45th also made their call before noon. A minor note of disappointment to the first day was that Allen had not yet landed his artillery or his armor — if the light vehicles of the cavalry recon squadron could be considered armor. The engineers had been more successful, for all their angle dozers were ashore and clearing obstacles.

Guzzoni responded immediately to the Allied invasion. He called on the 15th Panzers to move east to meet the 3rd Infantry, and at noon of D-day, the Herman Goering Division struck the Big Red One. Patton responded to the pleas of Allen and Bradley and released the one regiment of the 1st Infantry that had been the floating reserve (a buzzword learned from the Marines fighting in the Pacific). The armor of the Goering Division was far too much for the puny anti-tank measures that could be offered by the infantrymen or the paratroops, but the naval guns of the cruisers and destroyers in the water off the landing beaches could, and did, hit and disable the German Tiger tanks. They were able to stem the advance against the beleaguered 1st. The Axis determined to neutralize the naval anti-tankers, and the following morning, July 11, they sent wave after wave of fighter-bombers to strafe and bomb the naval vessels. They met with some success, for they sank an anchored ammunition ship and encouraged the naval combat vessels to up-anchor and make for safer water.

On the 11th, Patton was, as usual, roaming the front, encouraging here and there, and, sometimes, creating controversy. On this day he came upon a battalion of the 1st Infantry Division that was preparing to attack a position held by ground forces of the Italian Coastal Division, which had fallen back just out of Gela. The position the 1st was about to assault was, according to Patton's reasons, important to the effort to resist the thrusts of the Herman Goering Division. Patton summarily ordered the 1st to strike immediately, but the attack, which Patton witnessed, came to naught. Artillery support, which had been awaited, had not been used to keep the German heads down. The battalion suffered, and as expected, the word of Patton's direct order to the battalion commanding officer made its way up through regiment to division to corps. Bradley was furious with Patton's meddling and told him so. Patton, chastised, apologized and promised never again to interfere with Bradley's troops. But that evening, Patton reported to Eisenhower that Bradley needed to be more aggressive, implying that he, Patton, was having to do some of the work for the Corps and Division Commanders. Bradley never forgot this insult.

Before the invasion, during planning, Eisenhower had approved Patton's and Major General Matthew Ridgway's request that airborne troops be parachuted onto the beach to augment infantry on the ground. Ridgway did demand assurance that the aircraft and parachuting troops would be granted "safe conduct" from the surface anti-aircraft gunners. He received this assurance from all Commanders down to division level, and only then did he agree to make the drop.

The night of the drop — July 20 — was cloudless and breathless, and at the time of the drop, the Luftwaffe had made its nightly run and departed. All was in readiness for the 82nd Airborne Division parachutists. The lead flight of C-47 transports crossed the shore and headed for Gela, where the troops were to be dropped, when suddenly an American anti-aircraft gun on a Navy ship opened up. The fire was followed by every other gun on the beach and in the harbor. The besieged C-47 pilots tried evasive action, for they were already too low to save themselves by gaining altitude. They plunged onward through shot and shell and dropped their parachutists, who were immediately the targets of a shooting gallery from ground guns, small arms, rifles, and machine guns of the infantry they were coming to reinforce. Of the 144 planes that came forth from Tunisia, 22 failed to return, and many who did return bore the wounds of their adventure. A later count revealed airborne casualties at more than 20 percent.

The resulting accusations, recriminations, and righteous indignation did little to redress the results of the fiasco. The Navy, insisting that it was in a period of transition, held to its lofty view that in the past, any aircraft that had flown over Navy ships had been the enemy, and Navy gunners were simply reacting as would be expected of them. These lame denials flew in the face of the careful and repeated notifications, given to all surface personnel before the drop, that a friendly drop was to take place. Furthermore, the time and place of the drop had also been given to the anti-aircraft gunners who were participants in the turkey shoot.

Never again did airborne troops trust to fly over Navy ships. It is possible that the U.S. Navy killed more American troops than it did Axis troops in the whole Sicilian campaign.

Meanwhile, the 1st Infantry Division was fighting for its life, having been hit hard by the Herman Goering Division. Prior to the invasion, Patton had persuaded General Eisenhower to substitute the 1st Division for the green 36th Division. According to Bradley, this substitution saved the beach area at Gela, for, as he has written in *A General's Story*, "Only the perverse Big Red One with its no less perverse commander was hard and experienced enough to take that assault in stride."

During the assault of the 1st by the Herman Goering, Bradley asked Allen, who was "dog-tired," if he had everything in hand; Allen assured him that he had. Not long after this assertion, Allen got a call from Roosevelt, with the 26th Infantry, who said that if the Germans were to be stopped, it would be necessary to get some anti-tank guns firing on the Tigers. Allen knew Roosevelt well enough to know that he really meant just that. He responded and got on his command-net phones and told everyone with any gun whatsoever, even the artillery howitzers (which could of necessity be depressed — that is, the high trajectory could be lowered — to fire as guns) to come to the aid of the 26th. And they began to assemble in behind the beleaguered 26th infantrymen who had the courage to hunker down in their foxholes and let the Tigers go past, for they had nothing with which to stop them. But the waiting artillery, and for once the Americans, had a turkey shoot with Tiger tanks as the targets. More than half of the attacking tanks were destroyed; the remainder sensibly retreated. Later in the afternoon, the Tigers returned, but the artillery still had their muzzles depressed, and the naval guns also joined in, so that the turkey shoot of the morning was repeated. Those tanks not destroyed took to the hills, not to return during the Sicilian campaign.

Guzzoni began to sense that he could not drive the Allies into the ocean, and he turned to the strategy of establishing a defensive line from Enna to Catania. The 15th Panzer Division was soon to arrive and would take its place alongside the Herman Goering Division. In reserve was to be the newly arrived 29th Panzer Division, which, having just come from Italy, was to be the strengthening factor that would result in a stalemate in Sicily.

But Bradley had a new problem to deal with — Patton. After having made a very abbreviated visit to the Canadian area of the 8th Army, General Eisenhower had returned to Malta, yet unaware of the paratroop turkey shoot by the Navy and anti-aircraft. When the report of the debacle came to Patton, he dutifully forwarded it to Eisenhower. After reading the report, Eisenhower could feel his own skin blistering from the frying he might get from the American press some day, maybe even now. Hastily he sent Patton a scathing cable admonishing him to cut someone's head off and to conduct an inquiry to ascertain if fault could be found. More Bradley/Eisenhower justice was afoot, against which the U.S. general officers did not seem inoculated.

At or about this time, General Montgomery, of the 8th, conceived a stunning plan. Lieutenant General Sir Oliver Leese's XXX Corps on the left of the XIII Corps had not been stopped, as the XIII Corps had been before Catania. As Leese could seemingly make good progress, why not let him run with the bit, down the road from Siracusa to Caltanissetta and from there take Enna? Montgomery thought this was a splendid idea. Bradley thought it selfish and egotistical, when he realized that Montgomery had already set the corps in motion and nothing could stop it, save the Germans. Bradley fumed, probably because he hadn't thought of something so rare before Montgomery beat him to it. As it happened, by the time British General Alexander knew about the movement, Leese was already in motion. To Alexander, it seemed like a good idea because it might just give him fertile terrain for a series of victories that would end by taking Messina. Montgomery convinced Alexander (or did he tell him?) that he was already on the road and to turn back would be a loss of face not only for Montgomery but also for Alexander, who couldn't even control his own countrymen. So Alexander acquiesced and appeared to have given prior approval to the plan.

The more serious consequence of the use of the road by Leese was that this denied its use to any of the divisions of the II Corps. The order to limit the use of the Siracusa/Caltanissetta road to the British had been received by George Patton at 7th Army Headquarters with no more than an acknowledgment and a passing-on of Alexander's orders to Bradley. Bradley believed this meek attitude of Patton's was the result of the recent dressing-down that Patton had received from Eisenhower regarding the paratrooper-friendly fire disaster. The hatred that Patton showed for the British was a pole apart from Eisenhower's love, and Patton believed that Ike was just looking for an excuse, any excuse, to can him. Whatever the reason, Patton stood quietly by and watched while American divisions turned 180 degrees and relinquished ground that they had won, because in order to find a road on which they could advance, they were forced, literally, to back up.

General Bradley was furious. In order to accomplish what Alexander had directed, it was necessary for Bradley to have the 45th Division — then on the right flank of the 1st Division and shy of the road that Leese was calling his own — pull back, pass through the interior of the 1st, and assume a new position on the left flank of the 1st, leaving the 1st as the right flank of the "right hook" that the American Army had hoped to exert against Messina. Together with the other American units, the 45th Division would have to pursue a course of attack toward Palermo northwest rather than northeast toward Messina.

Regrouped and alert, the 7th Army was, at the time, capable of strong offensive activity, and Patton intended that it have such a role in a bold offensive move. He created a new corps from the 3rd Division, the 2nd Armored Division (Darby's Rangers — an elite infantry strike force), and a regiment of the newly arrived 9th Division, and he put Major General Geoffrey Keyes in command and set them to planning to take Palermo. But this scheme was soon thwarted when Alexander directed that the 7th would assume the role of protecting the left flank of the British 8th. This was too much for the angry Patton. On July 22 he confronted Alexander and Eisenhower, both in Tunis, and presented the reasoning that it was politically inexpedient for the 7th Army not to have equal glory with the 8th. The case was made, and both Eisenhower and Alexander approved. Patton, with his marching orders in hand, returned to Sicily, and four hours later the new corps began the attack that would ultimately take Palermo. Surprisingly, the formal orders from Alexander, which came the day after the attack had been launched, called on the 7th Army to attack north to secure the coast, and only after doing that was it free to strike toward Palermo! Supposedly, Patton's Chief of Staff, General H. R. Gay, who received the order, withheld it from Patton's eyes until Palermo was within grasp. For this, Gay was praised. Had the withholding of the order been something that displeased Patton, Patton would have wanted Gay to be shot.

Bradley's II Corps was now left with the enviable task of racing to the north coast, protecting the left flank of the 8th Army, and, as a final challenge, taking Enna. (Leese had dropped this task into Bradley's lap so that he could concentrate on Mt. Etna.) Bradley did what was expected and took Enna, for which, in the press, the Canadians were mistakenly credited. Meanwhile, Patton's foot soldiers of the 3rd Infantry, the 82nd Airborne, and the Rangers walked all the way to the outskirts of Palermo, the 2nd Armored bringing up the rear. When the "entry in triumph" was at hand, Keyes, the makeshift Corps Commander, gave the glory to the armored vehicles of the 2nd — or was it Patton's order that gave the tankers the privilege of taking Palermo? The 45th Division, led by Major General Troy Middleton, reached the outskirts of Palermo, but as Patton wanted to capture the city "his way," the Thunderbirds were waved off by Bradley so that the 2nd could take the city. The 45th did, however, reach the north coast at Termini Imerse, 30 miles east of Palermo, on July 23rd.

Allen, though, was not having such luck. The Germans to his front were not cooperating, as they were everywhere else on the island. These Germans were fighting. The Big Red One advanced as far as Petralia, north of Enna some 20 miles, and was stopped there by ferocious and tenacious troops of the Herman Goering Division. Montgomery's six divisions were stalled before Mt. Etna facing three German divisions, and they did not have enough advantage to dislodge them. And so it was decreed by Alexander that the original plan would be returned to — that of pointing both the British and the Americans toward Messina and urging them on. The 45th, which was on the north coast, and the 1st, which was to its right flank, took parallel roads in their quest. The 45th advanced eastward to San Stefano, nearly half the distance to the prize, while the 1st advanced but to Troina, a third of the way home. And there both were stopped.

At about this point in the campaign, Bradley decided to rest the 45th and the 1st, relieving them in the line with the 3rd and the 9th. Allen insisted that the 1st be allowed to take Troina before relief and Bradley agreed, giving him two of the 9th Division regiments to help in the assault.

The 1st Division was before Troina and the might of the Herman Goering Division and elements of the 15th Panzer Grenadier Division. Both sides were inclined to fight, and this they did. For seven full and tiring days, the 1st attacked again and again, and each time they were repulsed. Bradley has written that he found it necessary to take tactical command of the division, for their situation was in such shape that they needed an experienced person to assume leadership — this from a lieutenant general who had never commanded troops in combat. It is much easier to criticize if one begins command at the corps level, for there is little or no true contact with troops. Most soldiers know who their Division Commander is and some know what army they are in and some of them know who commands the army, but very few know what corps they are in and almost none know who commands the corps. In the same way, few Corps Commanders really know what is going on ahead of their front division.

But the situation in Troina gave Bradley the cause célèbre for which he had bided his time; now he had a viable reason to sack Allen and Roosevelt. In his book *A General's Life*, Bradley piously wrote that relieving Allen and Roosevelt was one of his "most unpleasant duties" of the war. With light at the end of the Sicilian tunnel, and with the 1st Division having furnished more than its part of that light, and with Allen and Roosevelt having given Bradley all that he had hoped, it was time to get rid of them.

To leave them around longer could possibly mean the conclusion of the campaign and the end of excuses, no matter how feeble, to relieve them. So Bradley acted with bold determination. He did what he had wanted to do since the 1st had gotten him chewed out so badly by Eisenhower for the Tunisian caper, when the 1st had pillaged and looted its way across Tunisia and Algiers after the victory there.

Bradley, more than any other American Commander, was a sacker of generals. But he always managed to use up the doomed general before doing so. He closed his episodes on Allen and Roosevelt by again piously declaring that he was proud to have Allen serve him at Normandy (command the Timberwolf 104th) and regretting that Roosevelt (who won the Congressional Medal for leading a combat team in the Normandy landing) had died of a heart attack in his tent the night before he was to know that Bradley had intended him to head the 90th Division.

Chapter 6

Lucas at Anzio — the Limited Beachhead

*J**OHN PORTER LUCAS** was born in West Virginia in 1880 and graduated from the U.S. Military Academy in 1911, at which time he was commissioned a second lieutenant, posted to the 13th Cavalry Regiment in Columbus, New Mexico. He commanded the machine-gun troop that repulsed Pancho Villa in the raid of March 9, 1916. He rode with General John J. Pershing in the Punitive Expedition into Mexico in 1916-1917. In 1918, he*

went to France with the 33rd Infantry Division and was wounded in action at Amiens. Following hospitalization in London, he
returned to America.

The period between the wars saw Lucas at the Army War
College (1918), as professor of military science and tactics at
the University of Michigan (1919), at the Field Artillery School
at Fort Sill, Oklahoma, as a student and an instructor (1920-
1923), at the Command and General Staff School, Fort Leavenworth, Kansas (1924), and at Colorado Agricultural College
(1925-1929).

In 1929, he briefly commanded a battalion of the 82nd Field
Artillery and then attended the Army War College at Carlisle
Barracks, Pennsylvania, graduating in 1932. In 1936, he was
with the G-1 Division of the General Staff in Washington; he
spent a brief tour at Fort Sam Houston, Texas; he took a short
course at the Artillery School at Fort Sill; and, in December, he
took command of the 4th Field Artillery at Fort Bragg, North
Carolina. After serving with the 1st Field Artillery at Fort Sill,
he was promoted to brigadier general and Commander of Division Artillery of the 2nd Infantry Division at Fort Sam Houston
in 1940. In the summer of the next year, he became Division
Commander of the 3rd Infantry Division at Fort Lewis, Washington.

While training the division in landing techniques, Lucas became the amphibious expert of the Army. From April 1942 to
May 1943, he was Commanding General of the III Army Corps
at Fort McPherson, Georgia. He returned to combat as the personal representative of General Dwight D. Eisenhower in North
Africa and Sicily and brilliantly commanded the II Corps in
Sicily. He then commanded the VI Corps, and after leading it up
the land axis of Italy took it to the amphibious landing at Anzio.

Upon his relief, Lucas returned to the United States as
Deputy Commander and then Commander of the 4th Army, Fort
Sam Houston, 1945-1946. He then served as chief of an Army
Advisory Group at Nanking, China, during 1946-1948, and as
Deputy Commander of the 5th Army, Chicago, in 1948, in
which year he retired with the rank of major general. He died
in 1948 at the Great Lakes Naval Hospital, Illinois.

Recent history has proven that establishing a beachhead behind the lines, when fighting a peninsular war, can prove very successful. General Douglas MacArthur did so at Inchon in Korea in 1950, boldly defying odds, and the whole enemy front collapsed behind the beachhead.

In 1944, Lieutenant General Mark Clark and his superior, General Sir Harold Alexander of the British, were stymied before Rome. German Field Marshal Albert Kesselring had skillfully retreated north. To set the stage: Field Marshal Sir Bernard Montgomery had led the British 8th Army across the Strait of Messina on September 3, 1943, and the 8th had landed on the "heel" of the Italian boot at Taranto on the same day. Moving northward, they had linked with Clark's 5th U.S. Army, which came ashore at Salerno on September 9, 1943. The Allies had advanced northwest along the Italian peninsula until they came upon the Gustav (Hitler) Line, a fortified entrenchment running between the Gulf of Gaeta and just south of Ortona on the Adriatic. There the advance had stopped and remained stopped. Higher command demanded that something be done to begin the advance again. It was decided to make an amphibious landing at Anzio, some 30 miles south of Rome on the west coast.

General Alexander asked General Clark to prepare a scheme — OPERATION SHINGLE — to land behind the line and penetrate the Germans, which would make their position untenable and cause a retreat. It was intended that but one division make the beach assault and drive inland where there would be a hookup with the overland troops of Clark at or about the village of Frosinine.

As might be expected, there were several opinions among the Allied leaders concerning the appropriate strategy to follow in Italy. Free French General Charles de Gaulle and Russian leader Joseph Stalin favored an immediate invasion of France. British Prime Minister Winston Churchill leaned toward taking Rome and then entering southern France and/or the Balkans (to use his terminology, "the soft underbelly of Europe"). The Americans were much of the same mind as Churchill on Italy but favored a cross-channel invasion rather than one across the Adriatic.

As plans for the exercise progressed, there were those who questioned the chances of success. Major General Lucien Truscott, who commanded the U.S. Army 3rd Infantry Division, which was to make the Anzio landing, was dubious that the necessary linkup between the amphibious force and the northward advancing 5th Army could be made within the allotted

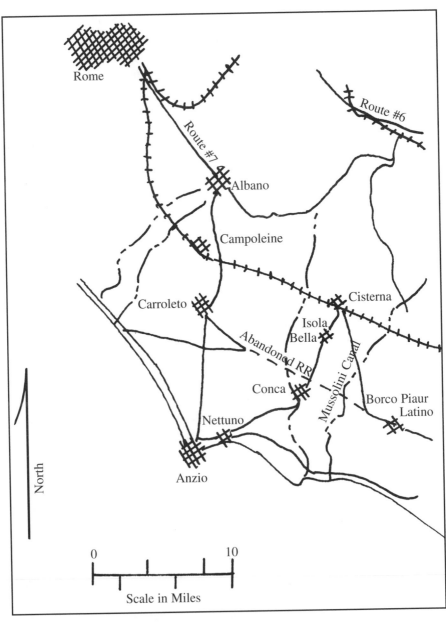

month and further believed that in the attempt to reach the hookup at
Frosinine, the 3rd Division would suffer inordinate casualties.

There was the additional complication of the availability of landing
craft to perform the Anzio operation. OPERATION OVERLORD, anoth-

Major General John P. Lucas was relieved of command of the VI Corps at Anzio because of his timidity at the outset of the operation and because he was unable to effect a breakthrough against Kesselring. (U.S. Army)

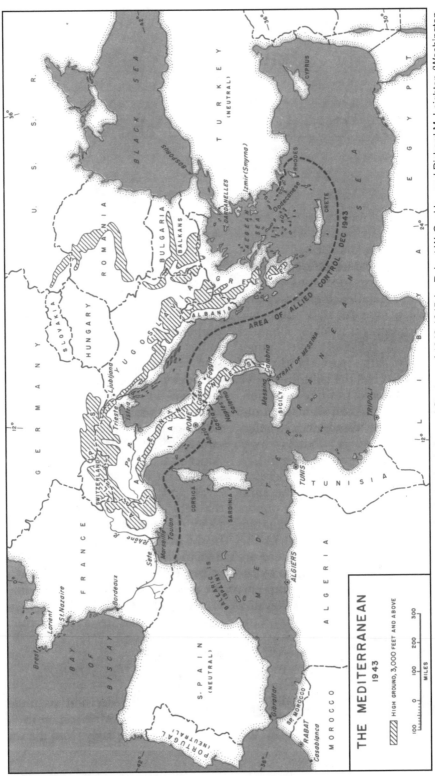

THE MEDITERRANEAN
1943

///// HIGH GROUND, 3,000 FEET AND ABOVE

MILES
100   0   100   200   300

From *U.S. Army in World War II: The War Department, Global Logistics and Strategy of 1943-1945*, by Robert W. Coakley and Richard M. Leighton (Washington, D.C.: U.S. Army, Office of the Chief of Military History, 1968), 174.

er cross-channel mission, would be staged in late spring or early summer, and there were not sufficient landing craft available to perform two such operations. There was thus the necessity to perform one, get it done, and then go to the other. Churchill, who enjoyed having a heavy hand in the immediacy of a theater, was keen on OPERATION SHINGLE, perhaps because he had hoped to erase the blot that the failure at Gallipoli in World War I had left on his ability as a great field captain. (In retrospect, it seems that Churchill never really believed that the Allied troops operating in Italy in 1915 were fighting as hard as they should, for if they were to fight but a bit harder, the Germans would roll right up the peninsula.) Churchill was the principal proponent for Anzio, and though it was shelved several times, he always managed to bring it to the fore.

Almost on direct line between the right flank anchor of the Gustav Line (the Gulf of Gaeta) and the proposed beachhead at Anzio were terrain features that the student of history will recognize immediately. Some of these rather familiar names, though unknown and unremarkable at the time of planning of SHINGLE, were the Via Appia (Highway 7), Monte Cassino, the Liri Valley (later named the Purple Heart Valley by the Americans), and the Rapido River.

It was 60 miles from the front to Anzio and 35 to the selected meeting place of Frosinine. It was thought that the distance should be lessened prior to the time of the amphibious assault at Anzio, so the American 5th Army began what was to become some of the bloodiest attacks of the American Army during World War II.

At the time the Anzio exercise was being planned and was about to take place, the order of battle in Italy had British Field Marshal Alexander in command of the theater, with the American 5th Army commanded by Lieutenant General Mark Clark and comprised of two corps — the II Corps, commanded by Major (soon to be Lieutenant) General Geoffrey Keyes, and the VI Corps, commanded by Major General John P. Lucas. Available to Clark were the 3rd, 36th, 45th, and 34th Infantry Divisions, the 82nd Airborne Division, and the 1st Armored Division. Other Allied troops were part of the British X, XIII, and V Corps, which commanded in total the 46th, 56th, and 78th Infantry Divisions, the 1st British Airbourne Division, the 1st Canadian Division, the U.S. 7th Armored, the French Corps (comprised of the 2nd Moroccan Division and the 3rd Algerian Division; later added was the 4th Mountain Division), the Polish Corps (comprised of the 3rd Carpathian Division), and the late-arriving

U.S. 85th and 88th Infantry Divisions. The odds in Italy were 18 to 7 in favor of the Allies.

Opposing were the Germans — Oberefehlshaber South (OB SUD), a command unit controlling several army groups, commanded by Field Marshal Albert Kesselring, and the 10th Army, commanded by Colonel General Heinrich von Vietinghoff, which included the XIV Panzer Corps, comprised of the 15th and 16th Panzer Divisions and the Herman Goering Division, and the LXXVI Corps, having the 26th Panzer Division, 29th Grenadier (Panzer) Division, and 2nd Parachute and 3rd Panzer Grenadier Divisions. These troops were assembled almost overnight by Kesselring, giving testimony to his logistic insight as well as to his persuasive ability. He had the unenviable task of convincing hard-pressed commanders to part with troops that they certainly believed critical to their well-being.

General Ernest J. Dawley had been sent by Washington to General Dwight D. Eisenhower to command a corps, and for this, Eisenhower was not happy. General Mark Clark accepted Dawley with somewhat more enthusiasm, but in September 1943, while on the Sele River offensive, Clark discovered that Dawley, then commanding the VI Corps, had not covered his left flank and had, in Clark's view, put the corps in jeopardy. With the approval of Alexander, Eisenhower, and General George C. Marshall, Clark relieved Dawley and replaced him with Major General John P. Lucas, who had been a deputy to Eisenhower in North Africa and had subsequently commanded the II Corps before General Geoffrey Keyes.

The events that led to the Anzio beachhead all pointed to the priority the Italian campaign held in the overall scheme. Eisenhower had told Alexander to expect no more than the fewer than 20 divisions that he was to finally receive. Yet, the Allies clamored for Rome. Hitler had considered securing a better-positioned line north of Rome, but Kesselring dissuaded him, asserting that he, Kesselring, could hold Alexander indefinitely on the defensive positions south of Rome.

OPERATION SHINGLE was about to become reality. Part of the need for this bold thrust was to keep the Germans busily engaged in Italy so that they would not withdraw forces from this theater and transfer them to the English Channel coast defense in anticipation of the forthcoming invasion.

In preparation for the linkup between the Anzio forces and those moving up the peninsula, Clark ordered Ernest Walker's 36th Infantry Division Texans to cross the Rapido River. In his book *Anzio: The Edge of Disas-*

Shore landing area at the Anzio beachhead. (U.S. Army Signal Corps)

Troops of the amphibious landing at Anzio. (U.S. Army Signal Corps)

ter, William Allen succinctly tells the story of the Rapido. Almost nothing went right in the attempt to assault the river. Engineer teams slipped across before the assault and cleared mine fields in select approaches. But after the engineers departed, the Germans left their trenches and relaid the mines. The far bank approaches were under constant observation and incessant artillery fire. More than half of the engineer assault boats were damaged before they were launched or failed to reach the far shore. Because of a quirk in Walker's system, the supporting engineer company, which had practiced an assault with the 142nd Infantry (of the 36th Infantry Division), found to their surprise that they were not ferrying the well-known regiment but a group of strangers — the 141st Infantry, whom Walker had judged more "combat ready and rested" than the regiment with whom the engineers had trained. The night before the assault, Walker wrote in his diary, "We might succeed, but I do not see how we can." After the war, the Texas Legislature persuaded the U.S. Congress to investigate the Rapido crossing (that is, Mark Clark). The Secretary of War at the time, Henry L. Stimson, wrote that Clark had exercised sound judgment, but this is perhaps not altogether true. He exercised rather poor judgment in entrusting the crossing to Walker. Yet, the Rapido was on the road to Frosinine where the Anzio forces were to meet the mainland advancing troops. It had to be crossed.

In his written instructions to Clark, Alexander indicated that the objective of the Anzio mission was to cut the communications of the enemy and to threaten the rear of the German XIV Corps. Though the Anzio operation was certainly not planned with the grim reality of the Rapido action in mind, it was executed with the full awareness that the so-called linkup probably would not happen as it had been planned and that rather the Anzio affair might take the heat off the Gustav Line and even divert the attention of Kesselring from his series of defensive successes — Rapido and Monte Cassino.

Eisenhower, in *Crusade in Europe,* noted that Anzio "paid off handsomely," yet in the early stages it developed as his Headquarters had expected. The landing craft that were to be transferred to England remained in the Mediterranean to provide "rapid reinforcement for the hard pressed troops at Anzio." Fortunately, he added, this did not affect OVERLORD. However, the forces at Anzio had to be built up and fought under adverse conditions. And, without doubt, the move convinced Hitler of our commitment to the Italian campaign as a "major operation," because he

Allied supply dump at water's edge, Anzio beachhead. (U.S. Army Signal Corps)

The terrain that lay before Lucas at Anzio. (U.S. Army Signal Corps)

brought in eight divisions — which turned out, said Eisenhower, to be a "great advantage to the Allies elsewhere."

Clark, in his instructions to General Lucas, ordered him to seize and secure a beachhead in the vicinity of Anzio and to advance on the Colli Laziali (the Alban Hill area south of Rome). Perhaps these were interpreted by Lucas as a sequence of priority, that is, seize first, then secure, and finally advance.

John Lucas had risen on the western front in 1918 and had ended World War I commanding an infantry battalion. Eisenhower had selected him as his personal deputy for the North African campaign. Lucas assumed command of the II Corps in Sicily in the summer of 1943 when General Omar Bradley left for a higher calling. In a short time, Lucas was transferred to the more active VI Corps, and he "fought" this unit with distinction up the peninsula. Anzio would give him the opportunity to operate almost independently and at a peer level with Clark, whose troops he would be trying so desperately to reach. In his diary, Lucas was quite candid. Fred Sheehan, in *Anzio, Epic of Bravery,* notes that Lucas had written, "This whole affair has a strong odor of Gallipoli and apparently the same amateur [Churchill] was still on the coach's bench." He also wrote, "Apparently Shingle has become the most important operation in the present scheme of things." Indeed, Churchill had been quoted as saying that it would astonish the world and would certainly frighten Kesselring. To this, Sheehan indicates that Lucas said he felt "like a lamb being led to the slaughter." He noted that he had but a minimum of "ships and craft," that he could only get a "weak" force ashore in a hurry, and he did not have enough artillery — though he would have more than adequate air support. According to Lucas, with just one week of good weather, he could succeed. The Germans were thought to be "fleeing in disorder," and the Allies had been advancing against them "with comparative ease."

Lucas maintained that he had written these words before the fact. If we are to believe this, we should look at them in the light of what happened and also in the light of what might have been had the operation been a great and immediate success. Had it succeeded, and gloriously, would Lucas have admitted his hesitations and that it was others who had driven him to success at Anzio? Doubtful. It is more likely that he was "Monday morning quarterbacking" and giving credence to the belief that Anzio was, even after the victory in Italy, a bad piece of strategy. If it was indeed so, and if Lucas had perceived that a debacle was about to occur, it would seem that he, a major general, could have extricated himself from it with grace.

One might also wonder if, with such foreboding as Lucas felt, it was as likely that he would be successful. Who would a soldier rather have lead him — the one who believes he will win or the one who does not believe he will win? The answer is too obvious. An observer of Lucas noted that he seemed "more impressed" by the difficulties than by the opportunities. Surely the individual who wrote these words did so after Lucas had left Anzio for good, not before he landed troops there.

The coastline west of the Italian peninsula was comprised of a series of crescents anchored on headlands (prominences), which secured the beginning of the crescent and terminated it as well. The littoral drift was from north to south, and there were gently sloping beaches with a three-foot tide. Sea turbulence was not as great in the west as in the east, on the other side of the peninsula. Anzio was situated on just such a prominence with the town of Nettuno to the immediate south. To the north some 30 miles were the southern boundaries of the capital of Rome. A coastal road ran northwest and southeast from the headland of Anzio. North from the village was the road to Albano; beside the road was a railroad that veered off to Rome at the station of Campoleone. From Nettuno, the village just south of Anzio, there were two roads to the east, one southeast along the coast and one northeast to the village of Conca and thence to the village of Cisterna.

The land to the south and east of Anzio had been marsh, before being drained in Fascist land reclamation programs. The main drainage structure was the Mussolini Canal that ran north and northeast, pointing toward the village of Cisterna and lying between the villages of Conca and Latina. It was a significant drainage structure and had the characteristics of a major river. It was an obstacle that required an assault crossing performed by combat engineers.

The wooded terrain to the northeast was intersected by many deep and narrow gullies carved into the volcanic soil, which was amenable to vertical sides. Through the town of Albano, 15 miles to the north, there was the famed Route 7, the Appian Way, which was the very pride of Italian engineers. Farther to the east was Route 6, which was paralleled by a railroad and which was also considered something of a design and construction achievement.

At the time when OPERATION SHINGLE was being planned,

Churchill showed his heavy hand again and again. Lucas, of the VI Corps, and Truscott, of the 3rd Division, thought that a full-scale rehearsal should be done by participants to train or reacquaint them with the various functions that were likely during the actual amphibious landing and the establishment of the beachhead. Churchill thought this absurd. Mark Clark finally intervened, and the rehearsal took place. Then, both Truscott and Lucas expressed concern due to the high number of untrained recruits in their units. Churchill, however, is alleged to have said, "One experienced officer or non-commissioned officer in a platoon is sufficient."

In the early hours of January 22, the landings at Anzio went without a hitch. The British, under Major General William Penney, landed north of Anzio with the objective of cutting the road to Albano. Anzio proper was encircled by the Ranger units under Colonel William O. Darby, who had the additional support of a parachute infantry battalion and a chemical mortar battalion. To the east, the 3rd Division, under Truscott, came ashore three regiments abreast and moved to secure bridges over the Mussolini Canal as well as to secure the road to Cisterna. The 504th Parachute Regiment, Corps Reserve, came ashore behind the 3rd while the entire British 1st Division remained on board ships as part of a floating reserve.

A noisy barrage preceded the assault landing, which seemed to stir up more soil than enemy. There was hardly any resistance! From his command ship a few miles offshore, General Lucas signaled General Clark that the landings had been made, the weather was perfect, and there was no significant opposition.

That Field Marshal Kesselring had gotten word of the landing became all too apparent the following day. In order to respond to the amphibious assault, it was necessary that he find and bring to bear forces to counter the invasion. By redirecting the roles of units he could summon, he was able, in half a day, to cause 11 German divisions and supporting units to start moving to Anzio. Most impressive were the responses of the 715th Division (from France) and the 114th Division (from Serbia), which arrived on the scene in less that a week.

But before the opposition to the invasion was felt by the VI Corps, it faced unobstructed terrain. At the time of the initial landing, the corps could have chosen any terrain (within driving time from the beachhead) to defend against that fateful day when Kesselring would come roaring down with his 11 divisions and supporting troops. But apparently General Lucas thought everything was fine and harbored no idea of expanding the territory over which he held domain. Recent historians have written that regardless of what terrain Lucas might have tried to secure, it is conceivable that he did not try to advance far enough to keep the beach, and command center, from being under the fire of medium artillery. Sheehan notes that Kesselring is reported to have said that on the initial day of the landing, the Allies

> did not conform to the German High Command's expectation. Instead of moving northward with the first wave to seize the Alban Mountains, they limited their objective, occupying but a small beachhead. During the time that they took to prepare for a breakout, sufficient German troops had arrived to prevent them from doing so.

The first objective of the 3rd Division was the far bank of the Mussolini Canal, and this was achieved in several places by the division's Cavalry Recon Troop on January 24. During the first night of occupying these positions, the troop was fallen upon by the Herman Goering Division, and all the crossings were taken back. Later the next day, and after some heavy artillery fire supported their attack, the 30th Infantry Regiment regained positions lost by them and by the cavalrymen, but not without heavy casualties. The very first attack and counterattack were previews of what was to come.

The front, on D+1, January 23, began at the sea on the left flank and was held by the British. This anchor was ten miles northwest of Anzio. Thence, the line ran due east to the Anzio/Albano road, where the American forces began. Their line (three times the length of the British) ran southeast to the Mussolini Canal and then down the canal to the sea. On this day, more reinforcements arrived to bolster the Allied effort, among them the 36th Engineer Regiment. Soon the first elements of the 45th Division began to arrive. The 1st Division launched an attack to capture Campoleone, the railroad junction of the two routes that converged to Rome. The 3rd Division set its sights on Cisterna, on the railroad south, and on the famed Route 7 to Rome.

General Truscott, of the 3rd U.S. Division, wanted desperately to secure his objective of Cisterna and proposed to Lucas that he be relieved of the responsibility of ten miles of front by causing the 1st to slide to the left and inserting the newly arrived 179th Regiment of the 45th in place of the

3rd so that the 3rd would be free to launch an attack to the north. But Lucas was not yet ready to launch an attack and chose to wait for the arrival of the 1st Armored Division before beginning a corps-coordinated offensive.

Air observation was certainly lacking in the Allied effort. Lucas did not know that there were but a few scattered battalions of the German army between Anzio and Rome for several days after the invasion, and thus the corps did not attack. This allowed Kesselring plenty of time (though he did act with remarkable speed) to assemble troops to counter the attacks that would eventually come. At the first dawn, Kesselring had put the German effort to contain the Anzio beachhead under the command of the 1st Parachute Corps, but he was able to assemble more troops than this Headquarters could oversee and command. He remedied this by bringing in General August von Mackensen who headed the German 14th Army, which had been stationed in Verona.

By D+3, the 25th, Alexander was concerned with the inactivity of the VI Corps and told Clark to get Lucas moving. Though the prodding by Clark was gentle at first, by the 27th, D+5, Clark had become insistent that Lucas attack toward Cisterna. Finally, Lucas planned a corps assault on D+7, but a delay was necessary because the 1st Armored Division (only recently entirely assembled) was not quite ready to begin an attack.

The attack was to be two-pronged, with the 3rd Division directed north; its objective was to cut Highway 7. The 1st Infantry Division would attack north to Campoleone, and the 1st Armored would pass through the 1st and swing right to secure the Alban Hills. On the left, the British sought to secure the railroad bridge on the road to Campoleone.

On the fateful day of D+7, January 29, just as the Allied attack was beginning, the German air force struck Anzio. It pulverized the beachhead, shattered supply dumps, and sunk several vessels in the harbor. The Germans first had come to life on the ground, with the attack of the Herman Goering Division. Then, the Luftwaffe of Reichmarshal Herman Goering was spoiling an attack.

Lucas put the 36th Engineers on the left along with the British, and the 179th of the 45th Division replaced the 504th Parachute Infantry Regiment, which was to be used in the assault on Cisterna. But, the British attack was not able to secure even the line of departure (LD) of the attack. The abandoned railroad bed between Latina and Patiglione was to be the LD for the 1st Armored. They, too, never got there but became mired in the mud as soon as they left the hardtop. Finally, the British were able to get moving toward Campoleone and at least got past the "flyover." At this point, January 30, D+8, General Lucas decided the attack wasn't going at all as planned and that Major General Ernest N. Harmon, Commander of the 1st Armored, simply couldn't operate off the road. So he changed the plan.

Henceforth, the British were to press to secure the intersection of the roads at Carroceto. When this was accomplished, Harmon would use the secured road to take his armor northwest to Carroceto and then swing north on the Anzio/Albano highway. All of these plans were put into effect, but the Allies were severely beaten back by the Germans. At the close of January 31, D+9, Lucas realized that Harmon's tanks could not penetrate the German defense and pulled the 1st Armored back into corps reserve. The British were having some success in their effort to capture Campoleone; they had penetrated almost to the railroad connecting Cisterna and Campoleone.

To the right of the VI Corps was the debacle of a bold and failed attack. Darby's Rangers had spearheaded the attack of the 3rd Division that had begun a few hours after midnight on the morning of January 30, D+8. They had moved northeast on the road from Conca to Cisterna. During the dark of early morning they were seemingly undetected and moved without attracting enemy resistance. But daylight found them confronted by a number of self-propelled guns blocking the way. The Germans opened up with direct fire, and as the Rangers tried to pass undetected, Germans on both sides of the road fired on them from the front and from both flanks. As this happened in the most inopportune location — one completely devoid of either cover or concealment — the German defenders took advantage of their favorable situation. By early morning, the American battalion had lost all but 6 of the 767 men who began the attack, and some of these were wounded. The remainder were either dead or captured.

Meanwhile, the 3rd Division was attempting to capture Cisterna by a parallel attack through Isola Bella. It, too, met with a most fierce resistance and stalled halfway to Cisterna. The other 3rd Division attack, alongside the Mussolini Canal, was successful in cutting the road to Cisterna and Velletri, but it could make no more progress. The strikes were resumed on the 31st, D+9, but met with no success. Again on the next day, assaults were attempted against the same objectives and using the same lines of attack, which, incidentally, were the only lines of attack available to the Allies. As it became apparent that the strike had stalled, the German 14th Army began to plan a counterattack aimed at eliminating the beachhead entirely.

General Clark had been castigated by British General Alexander, who had been chided by Lieutenant General Sir Henry Wilson (the Mediterranean Commander), who had been told by no less than Churchill that there was no possible reason for not having taken the towns of Cisterna and Campoleone while they were undefended. Clark responded to his dressing-down by moving his advance Headquarters to Anzio. He had to admit that the 1st and 3rd Divisions (a third of his total) were exhausted and needed time to recuperate. He also recognized that the Rangers were not suited to the tasks that had been given them, for, among other things, they were too lightly armed to counter the German thrusts against them. Furthermore, they were not trained, or capable, to fight as line infantry.

Allied Intelligence (American, at least) has always identified the lineup of the enemy by fragments of information pieced together (for example, asking a prisoner the name of his unit, seeing the shoulder patches of prisoners), and from these pieces the order of battle of the enemy has been put together. Such was done at Anzio with the help of 5th Army staff outside the beachhead. But Kesselring had committed troops from wherever he could find them, and thus units that represented only a fragment of a total wearing that insignia, or being in that unit, were put into battle. So, when Allied Intelligence began to put on a situation map all the units that had been identified, it appeared that the Germans had managed to achieve a miracle by putting more than 170,000 troops to oppose 90,000 Allied troops. Actually, however, the numbers at Anzio were about equal, German to American, for the shoulder patches of prisoners didn't tell the true story. But even with equal numbers, the Germans and Allies were destined to stalemate, for it takes superiority of at least one and one-half to be successful in attack, and both sides were trying to win by attacking.

General Clark had visited Lucas on D+8, January 30, and had noted in his diary that he had admonished Lucas, but had done so to "energize him to greater effort." Two days later, Lucas was visited by British General Alexander. Lucas later wrote of the two visits: "My head will probably fall in the basket — there are too many Germans here for me to lick." After conferring and discussing the situation they had just seen, Alexander and

Clark concluded that there were indeed "too many Germans" and ordered Lucas to take the defensive.

The Germans were about to take the offensive, but before they did they cleaned up the command jumble that had prevailed since they had summoned units to the invasion. The principal and complete elements — 3rd Panzer Grenadier; 26th Panzer; 4th Parachute; 65th, 71st, and 715th Infantries; and the Herman Goering Division — were supported by numerous artillery and special combat units commanded by two corps, the I Parachute and the LXXVI.

On the night of February 3, D+12, the Germans struck the salient that had been formed on the Albano road and just south of the railroad junction at Campoleone. It was defended by the British Guards Division. The assault was made on both shoulders simultaneously; the eastern attack made more headway. British counterattacks restored some of the lost positions of the morning, and when night fell the adversaries were about as they were when the attacks began. Lucas decided that the pronounced salient was a bit too inviting to the Germans and too difficult to defend by the British. He ordered a withdrawal to just north of Carroceto. The Germans had achieved a part of their objective — the dagger into their heart upward on the Albano road had been blunted and its thrust stopped. It would be three months before the Allies, advancing from victory on the Gustav Line, would hear of the breakout from Anzio.

Having been told by both Alexander and Clark to assume a defensive position, Lucas organized his troops on the line he then held and further defined a final beachhead defense to be fallen back to in good order should the pressure from the Germans become too great. By this time, Lucas had lost the spirit for victory on the Anzio front and was simply thinking of survival. To give substance to the order, the troops began what was to become the most elaborate defensive system set up in Europe by American troops. Bunkers, trenches, and redoubts of the heaviest construction possible, under battlefield conditions, were erected by the Allies. And they did have to put up with German attacks. On February 7, D+16, the first of several U.S. Army nurses was machine-gunned while scrubbing in an operation within the surgical tent of an evacuation hospital. Later, a German bomber, leaving the combat area, unloaded its bombs, and these inadvertently hit another American hospital. More than 100 were killed, including three nurses. February 7 also brought a resumption of Kesselring's attacks at the shoulders of the salient at Carroceto. The attacks continued for three days, during which the British lost the Carroceto station to the Germans, regained it, and then lost it again. The 3rd Division was not so busily engaged, as von Mackenson and the German 14th Army concentrated their efforts on the Albano/Anzio highway and, specifically, Carroceto. On February 9, D+18, the attacks and resistances came to a halt and were to remain so until, after relieving the exhausted 1st, the 45th stormed the factory outside the village, attacking through the overpass. All day on February 12, D+21, it was give and take; but at day's end, both adversaries were about where they started.

During this time, Churchill was carping to Alexander that the Americans had 18,000 vehicles on the beachhead for more than 70,000 troops, or, by Churchill's reckoning, four men per vehicle. He was amazed that so many vehicles were needed in an area so small — no more than nine miles to ride at the most. In addition, there were many in the line of command who realized that the situation in Anzio was stagnant, probably because they, from Churchill on down, had failed to emphasize that it would be necessary to exploit any opportunity that might arise. Lucas had not gotten this word and had been content to establish the beachhead and hold it.

Dissatisfaction with Lucas was building with Churchill, Alexander, and finally Clark. Lucas sensed this; how could he not? On February 15, D+24, Sheehan states that Lucas wrote:

> I'm afraid that those topside are not satisfied with me. They are naturally disappointed that I have not chased the Hun out of Italy, but there was no military reason why I should have been able to do so.

When a representative of theater Commander Eisenhower visited him, Lucas was asked why he had not pressed on to Rome just after he landed. Lucas replied that to have done so would have been to invite attack on the corps, which would have been without flank protection and would have spelled disaster, maybe even the loss of the entire corps. Furthermore, his orders did not instruct him to go seeking Rome.

General von Mackenson's strength was improving at this time. Though he returned the 71st Division to the army effort, he was supplemented by the 29th Panzer Grenadier Division, the 362nd Division from the north, and the 114th Division from Serbia. On the evening of February 15, D+24, the Germans began heavy shelling of the harbor at Anzio, the infantry rear, and up to and including battalion command. As the night lengthened, the barrage concentrated on front lines and the interdiction of the supply road net. At 6:00 a.m. on the 16th, D+25, following an intense artillery barrage, von Mackenson again attacked against the shoulders of the salient.

For five days, the German 14th Army spent its all trying to dislodge the VI Corps from around the concentration at Carroceto, including the factory and the overpass. At the end, the Germans had driven to the overpass, a scant three and one-half miles from Anzio and on the "final defense line." During this time, Clark had named Truscott as Deputy Corps Commander. This move was interpreted by Lucas as being a precursor to his removal. He wrote on February 17, the day of Truscott's appointment, "I think this means my relief." The very next day, before telling Lucas, Clark told Truscott that he would replace General Lucas as Corps Commander. For four more days, Lucas fought to stem the German tide and finally succeeded in doing so. On February 23, the day after the German advance finally ground to a halt for good, Clark relieved Lucas and appointed Truscott to continue the defense of Anzio.

Years later, Clark said that he perhaps waited too long to replace Lucas. It is thought that he did it not for the reason he has given — exhaustion — but because of a remark made by Alexander, who is alleged to have told Clark that they might be pushed back into the sea, "and that would be bad for both of us. You would be relieved of your command." The thought of being sacked himself was threat enough for Clark to heave his old friend Johnny Lucas.

As an aftermath, on May 21, the main front in Italy, the one in front of Monte Cassino, began to advance and with it the labored Anzio effort. By May 25, the II Corps of General Keyes and the VI Corps of Truscott met at a point on Route 7 (just a mile northwest of Latina, about 15 miles from the port of Anzio). The II Corps had traveled 42 miles to reach the meeting; VI Corps had traveled 6!

Had Lucas, with the beachhead forces he landed, tried to take the Alban Hills and, even more boldly, to take Rome, he would have been doing just what was wanted of him by both Churchill and Kesselring. One has but to consider how quickly the German troops were brought to the front to attack the beachhead to realize that a doubling of the radius of the perimeter (from 10 miles to 20 miles) would have doubled the front line and required at least twice the troops necessary to hold it than were needed to protect the perimeter that prevailed at the time of the furious German attacks. Churchill is to have said, "Anzio will astonish the world." How was he to know that this brilliant plan of his would come to no success and, for all its fanfare, have no significant effect on the outcome of the European struggle or that in Italy?

John Lucas returned to America without prejudice. He immediately took command of the 4th Army headquartered in Memphis, Tennessee. The responsibility of the 4th was to see to the preparation of the combat units then training in the United States and, if the need arose, command 4th Army troops to repel any invader of American shores. In 1946, Lucas was posted as chief of an American advisory group to Nanking and Chiang Kai-shek. There he remained until 1948, when he returned to the United States as Deputy Commander of the 5th Army in Chicago. He retired in 1950 and died in 1952.

Chapter 7

Smith *vs.* Smith, Army *vs.* Marines at Saipan

RALPH C. SMITH *was born in Omaha, Nebraska, in 1893 and attended Colorado State College before enlisting in the Colorado National Guard in 1916, from which he was commissioned second lieutenant and immediately promoted to first lieutenant. He entered Officers Training School at Fort Leavenworth, Kansas, and graduated in 1917. He saw short service on the Mexican border with the 35th Infantry and went to*

Major General Ralph Smith, the ill-fated commander of the U.S. 27th Infantry Division, who was relieved of command by Marine General Holland "Howlin' Mad" Smith. (U.S. Army Corps/Library of Congress)

France with the 16th Infantry. While he was in combat, he served with the 1st Infantry Brigade, the 4th Division, and the 7th Brigade. He was engaged at the Lunéville and Toul Sectors,

Cantigny, Aisne-Marne, St.-Michel, and the Meuse-Argonne. In the latter action he was wounded, for which he received the Purple Heart. He also held the Silver Star with Oak Leaf Cluster.

Before returning to the United States in 1919, Smith served with the American forces in Germany. For a year he was adjutant of the 2nd Infantry Brigade in Kentucky. In 1920, he spent the year as an instructor at the U.S. Military Academy before joining the 18th Infantry in New York and New Jersey. In 1923, he entered the Infantry School at Fort Benning, Georgia, and after his graduation in 1924, he remained as an instructor. In 1927, he entered the Command and General Staff School at Fort Leavenworth, Kansas, was graduated the following year, spent the next year at the Presidio of San Francisco, and returned to Fort Leavenworth in 1930 as an instructor at the Command and General Staff School. Four years later, in 1934, he entered the War College and graduated the following year. He then was chosen for the prestigious Ecole de Guerre in France.

In 1937 he served with the 29th Infantry at Fort Sill, Oklahoma. In 1938, as a full colonel, he became Chief of the Operations Branch, Military Intelligence Division (G-2) of the War Department General Staff, and in 1940, he became Chief of Plans and Training Branch of the G-2 Division. The next year he received his first star as brigadier general.

Upon the activation of the 76th Infantry Division at Fort George Meade, Maryland, he became Assistant Division Commander, and in 1942, he took the 27th Infantry Division to the Pacific, having been promoted to major general and Division Commander. After his adventure with Marine Lieutenant General Holland M. "Howlin' Mad" Smith, he commanded, for a short time, an unnamed infantry division in Hawaii.

Fluent in French, Ralph Smith became Military Attaché to the American Embassy in Paris until his retirement as a major general in 1946. In addition to his other decorations, he also held the Legion of Merit.

In August of 1941, Admiral Harold R. Stark, writing from Washington,

D.C., to Rear Admiral Husband Kimmel in Honolulu, expressed regret that nothing effective could be done to strengthen the defenses of Guam. He virtually conceded that the Japanese thrust, when it came, would take the island. He wrote a most profound epitaph to the island's impending fate caused by years of neglect, interestingly and principally by the United States Navy. "Dollars cannot buy yesterday," wrote Stark to Kimmel.

In less than half a year, Guam would be in the hands of the Japanese, and Kimmel would be disgraced as the man who slept while the Japanese planned and sunk his fleet. It is interesting that Harry Gailey, in his excellent book *The Liberation of Guam*, has stated, when writing on the inadequacy of Guam's defense, that Guam "was actually in better condition to resist an invasion in 1921 than it was twenty years later." Guam was unable to resist the Japanese invasion when it came on the morning of December 10, 1941. And from that day on, until the last of the Japanese resistance had been quieted (the Japanese forces formally surrendered bit-by-bit in the fall of 1945), the Americans were committed to the restoring of yesterday by the expenditure of countless dollars and many lives. Gailey has reported that the defense force for all of Guam on December 7, 1941, was composed of about 200 Marines commanded by a light (lieutenant) colonel, several hundred Navy personnel (unarmed and principally concerned with the infrequent arrival and departure of Navy ships and in tending to the old harbor oiler, the *Penguin*, and the three light patrol boats), and several hundred Guamanians who made up the indigenous defense force. The Japanese attacked Guam for two days, beginning on the 7th, with incessant aircraft bombing and strafing. Their purpose was unclear. Certainly they knew that the island was virtually undefended and would offer negligible resistance. Whatever damage would be done to the infrastructure would directly and immediately affect the Japanese conquerors. But, it was done.

Resistance from the island defenders was, for the most part, desultory. The *Penguin*, bearing the heavy defense armament (150-caliber machine gun), took to sea and fired until the gun crew had all been killed. Only then did the skipper scuttle her. Japanese infantry came ashore, first in the north, then the main force at about Agana, and, later in the day, the southern force (supposedly the main island attack force) at Agat. In the plaza in Agana, there was some spirited exchange before all became quiet and the fighting ended. Captain G. J. McMillan, U.S. Navy, Governor of the island

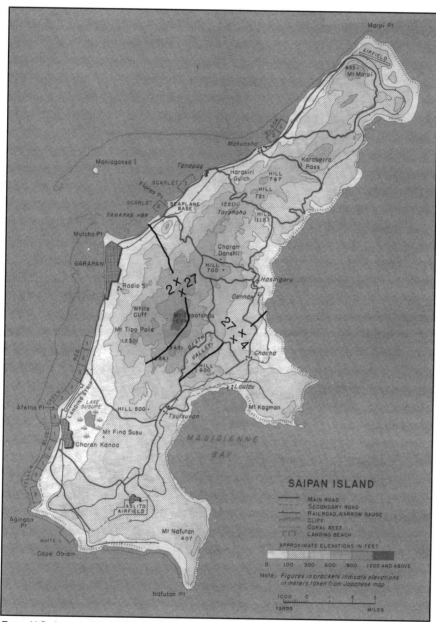

From *U.S. Army in World War II: The War in the Pacific, Campaign in the Marianas*, by Philip A. Crowl (Washington, D.C.: Dept. of the Army, Office of the Chief of Military History, 1960), Map II.

of Guam, surrendered the island to the Imperial Forces of Japan in the early morning of December 10, 1941. The first link in the chain of Honolulu, Wake, Guam, and Manila had been broken. More were to follow.

Hardly could the occupation by Japan be described as benign, but hardly could it compare in brutality to that which the Germans invoked on the Serbs or Poles, or which the Japanese invoked on the Koreans, the Filipinos, or the Chinese. At first, the Japanese tended to treat the newly conquered islanders with sternness, but not cruelty. There were harsh measures for violating any of the many rules of occupation that the captors promulgated.

About ten American military personnel had escaped capture when the island was overrun and were hiding in the hills. The Guamanians were particularly anxious to keep these men alive and free, for they were a final symbol of America, the only thing for them to cling to. So these men were carefully guarded, helped, and moved from place to place, ever ahead of the searching Japanese. Finally, this cat-and-mouse game in its simplest form proved too much for the occupiers, for the Americans were beginning to become the focus for Guamanian resistance. An edict went out that any Guamanian even suspected of aiding, housing, or even knowing the proximate whereabouts of one of these American servicemen would, if refusing to reveal information leading to their capture, be executed. Of course, anyone turning in information would be executed anyway. Such was the paranoia of the Japanese, once aroused. Of those Americans free and roaming, all were eventually captured save one — a serviceman named George Tweed who remained free during the entire occupation. He made his way to American ships offshore during the shelling of the islands preparatory to the U.S. invasion.

The Japanese commander of the defense of the island was Lieutenant General Takeshi Takashina. He had lost a considerable number of his intended defense force when the American destroyers sank troop-laden Japanese ships (the 29th Japanese Infantry Division lost 3,000 men in one sinking alone). But the artillery capabilities of the Japanese defenders were impressive. Two dozen 200-mm guns were strategically located around the island covering approaches, principally on the west where the Japanese were sure an attack would occur. The additional ten 150-mm seacoast guns and their smaller counterparts — two dozen 105-mms and a few fixed-mount 75-mms — made up the coastal defense. It has been estimated that at its peak, and before the American landings, Takashina had approximately 18,500 troops in total with which to defend the island.

Guam is approximately 35 miles long (in a northeast/southwest axis) and 10 miles in width. A massive ridge runs the length of the east coast. The countryside south of Agana is more mountainous than the north, which is gently rolling. To the south, at the time of the retaking, there was a perimeter road and but one transverse road, while in the north there was a handful of roads stemming from Agana and running to the two headlands on the north coast. Also, there was a road immediately across the island from Agana that accessed the east coast.

Guam was a prized American possession. But there were others, in the Marianas chain of islands, stretching 500 miles. From these islands the Japanese were supposed to be building a system of fortresses stretching across the Pacific. It is even rumored today that the Kansas aviatrix Amelia Earhart, who was last heard from as she was flying somewhere among these myriad of Pacific atolls in 1937, was shot down by the Japanese for flying too close to a Japanese military installation. If allowed to escape, they thought, she would surely go and tell Roosevelt, who would retaliate in some insidious way. (It may indeed be true that she was shot down by the Japanese, but it is more likely that she discovered that the supposedly heavily fortified Japanese island was not fortified at all. It is now the consensus opinion that in those years, Japan was bluffing.) And so when it was planned by America to retake Guam, it was thought logical to first retake Saipan, 300 miles north of Guam.

The two dominant figures in the area were Admiral Chester Nimitz and General Douglas MacArthur. As might be expected, MacArthur wanted to begin in New Guinea and move his conquests steadily northward until Japan itself was taken. From where he sat in Honolulu, Nimitz wanted to advance the war relentlessly west until Japan was taken. It was up to General George C. Marshall, Admiral Ernest J. King, and finally, President Franklin D. Roosevelt to choose one course or the other or to strike a compromise between the two. A compromise was chosen, and MacArthur continued to slug it out on the northern slope of New Guinea and in the Solomons at Guadalcanal while Nimitz struck at Tarawa in the Kiribati (2,300 miles south of Hawaii) and the Marshalls, Kwajalein, and Eniwetok. And next in Nimitz's line of advance were the Marianas, which included Guam and Saipan.

Of those called to active duty by Roosevelt at the beginning of the national defense alert, the 27th Infantry Division was the first unit to be sent overseas. They were posted to Hawaii early in 1942 for the purpose of defending the island against Japanese attack. The 27th was a National Guard unit from New York, with some units from Pennsylvania. Among the units integral to the division was the 165th Infantry Regiment, which had previously borne the designation 69th Infantry Regiment — the "Fighting 69th" of World War I fame. At the time of its transfer to Hawaii, the division was still organized as a square division, one having four of everything, including four infantry regiments — the 105th, 106th, 108th, and 165th. While in Hawaii, the units of the division were frequently posted to other units and to various islands. When it was determined to use the unit elsewhere, it was reassembled in Honolulu and received a new Commanding General, Major General Ralph Smith, recently the Assistant Division Commander of the 76th Division at Fort Meade, Maryland.

Ralph Smith was a soldier's soldier. He was a farm boy from Nebraska who had joined the National Guard in Colorado just as his new unit was nationalized in 1916 because of the crisis over Pancho Villa in Mexico. Through training he was commissioned and newly posted to the 1st Infantry Division, which was in the process of moving to France. He commanded a Browning Automatic Rifle (BAR) unit until he was recognized by a senior officer, General John Hines, who had known him from Mexican days. Asked to join a regimental staff — heady stuff for a new second lieutenant — he spent a time in training troops. Hines was himself picked to become the new Commanding General of the 4th Division and took Smith along as a member of the G-3 (the Operations section of the General Staff). Smith soon was promoted to major. He was lightly wounded in the arms and a leg, which forced him to spend the remainder of World War I in the hospital. He improved his ability to speak French during convalescence. After the Armistice, he rejoined Hines and remained in the occupation of Germany as a brigade adjutant until the unit was returned to the United States. Between the wars he taught French at West Point, attended the Sorbonne in France, and spent time at the Infantry School at Fort Benning, Georgia, the Command and General Staff School at Fort Leavenworth, Kansas, the Army War College at Carlisle Barracks, Pennsylvania, and the l'Ecole de Guerre in Paris. He then served on the General Staff in Washington. He was returning to duty at Fort Benning when he was rerouted and sent back to rejoin troops. It was from this assignment that he came to command the 27th Division. His manner to all who knew him was gentle. He has been remembered as a gentleman.

Holland M. "Howlin' Mad" Smith was a Marine, and he thought of himself as a "Marine's Marine." He was born in 1882 in rural Alabama. His father was a successful, appointed Alabama politician. Holland Smith graduated from the Alabama Polytechnic Institute in 1901 and then proceeded to law school, which he finished in the requisite two years. He went to Washington as a young and rather unsuccessful attorney to seek direct appointment to the Army, but he was turned down, a rejection that led to his life-long resentment of that service. Instead, he received a commission in the United States Marines. Before coming to plead for the commission, he had never even heard of the Marines. Yet he later spent a whole career acting as if that service was the true keeper of Utopia. During his early years in the Marine Corps, he served in China, Japan, Mare Island, and Nicaragua, and in Santo Domingo to quell the uprising. He remained as the Military Governor of Puerto Plata. When World War I came, he joined the new Marine brigade that, on the western front, was a part of the Army 2nd Division. During this posting, he was frequent in his denunciation of the Army, and he was an unimpressive staff officer. Though he saw service in Nicaragua and World War I, he was never exposed to artillery or small-arms fire. Returned from overseas postings, he attended the Marines School at Quantico and became heavily involved in amphibious warfare, which he had a part in shaping for the Marines. He crossed swords with Navy persons like Admiral Ernest J. King concerning the use of Marines in amphibious operations, and he missed what he perceived to be his due when he failed to command the 1st Marine Division.

In early 1942, the expert in the U.S. Navy on amphibious landings was Admiral Richmond Kelly Turner. In keeping with Navy tradition of letting the Marines in on everything (as long as they knew their place), Nimitz asked for a Marine amphibious officer and got Holland Smith. It was Howlin' Mad Smith who was to command the newly formed V Amphibious Corps, though he had never been in actual combat and had never commanded a unit higher than a rifle company.

General Ralph Smith had made several successful takings of Japanese-occupied islands — Tarawa and Kwajalein. Then he was charged with the taking of Saipan while his counterpart, H. M. Smith, took Guam. Previously, in the taking of Makin Island in the Gilberts, the 165th Infantry of Ralph Smith's 27th Division had served as a separate regimental combat team for H. M. Smith and the Marines. In this action, H. M. Smith had seemed pleased with the performance of the unit from the 27th; it seems that it was the unit's commander whom H. M. Smith disliked.

As an interesting side note, then-Major General Robert C. Richardson, the Army Administrative Commander in the Pacific, voiced a strong objection to General George C. Marshall regarding the practice of having Army units serve under the Marines or the Navy. He, like others, pointed to the fact that prior to creating just recently two amphibious corps, the Marines had no units larger than a division. Marine officers were not trained to command a mass of troops greater in size than a division. If the Marines needed a learning experience in corps command, let them learn it by using (and misusing) their own troops, not Army troops. As a result of the experiences learned in World War II, it is likely that the Marines will never again command mixed troops in a corps. It is further possible that Marines will not again be formed into a corps.

H. M. Smith's V Amphibious Corps was charged with the amphibious landing and taking of the island of Saipan, to occur on June 15, 1944. The 2nd and 4th Marine Divisions were to land in the vicinity of Charan Kanoa and Afetna Point and the 27th Division at Nafutan Point. As the Marine units moved ashore, they were to swing left to gain a route of advance on the major axis of the island. The Army's 27th, which by this time would have caught up with the Marines, would join them, and together the Marines and the Army would finish off the Japanese on the island. But the first obstacle to this plan was the disorderly way that the Navy landed the units of the 27th. Then once the chaos of landing was righted, the Japanese defenders on Mt. Nafutan put the southern landing objectives behind schedule. Units easily advanced east and west of the mountain, but the center was a strongly held position. H. M. Smith, who never once visited the scene to see firsthand, stormed and raged that anyone could take on the "200 Japs" that were holding up the invasion plans. Yet these Japanese troops, who numbered less than 200 in the mind of Holland Smith, left nearly 600 corpses on the mountain.

Meanwhile, the landings at Charan Kanoa had been going well until they, too, came upon terrain features held by "200 Japs" — Mt. Tapotchau and the ridge that would come to be known as Purple Heart Ridge. There the Americans were stopped. H. M. Smith decided to bring up the 27th Division to share with the 2nd and 4th the challenges that were on the front.

The two Marine divisions shifted right and left and permitted the 27th to come between them and take its place in the line on June 23. That day, immediately as they entered the line, the V Corps attacked. Modest gains were made by the 2nd Division along the coast, but none in front of Mt. Tapotchau. The 27th got nowhere, for they were being fired on by well-entrenched troops on both the mountain and on the ridge. The 4th Marine Division, on the right, seemed to have the rabbit's foot, for they had advanced halfway across the peninsula. The next day saw little better for the 27th, while the two Marine divisions made significant advances in their sectors.

An axiom learned by both the Army and the Marines is that when operating with friendly troops on your flanks, you are responsible, if possible, for keeping contact with and keeping up with the unit on your left flank. The Marine unit on the left flank of the 27th was engaged and occupied with Mt. Tapotchau and was inclined, if resistance permitted, to slide around the mountain to its left, while — if pressure allowed — the 27th would yield to the right. And so they did, and a gap occurred. Similarly, the 4th, on the right of the 27th, was having some comparative easy going and simply went off and left the 27th still struggling with Purple Heart Ridge.

When the Japanese defenders found the two gaps, they determined to take advantage of them. On June 25, the third night that the three divisions had been together, the Japanese attacked between the divisions — both gaps. They penetrated nearly 500 yards at each location and were only beaten back by strong counterattacks.

For Holland Smith, the performance of the 27th Division — after being between two superb Marine divisions for three days — confirmed to him that the 27th must have a new Commander. Finally, he had been given cause célèbre to fire Ralph Smith.

During the time that the 27th Division had been under Marine control in Saipan, no officer of the V Amphibious Corps had visited the front line at the location of the 27th to ascertain the nature of the terrain or to assay the concentration and utilization of enemy troops confronting the advance of the Division. Belatedly, on the very day that H. M. Smith was to relieve Ralph Smith, an officer of the corps' G-3 paid a visit to the front. On viewing the situation he said, "I had no idea that this was the situation that faced you. No wonder that you have had difficulty making progress. I'll go back to see if we can't send you some help." Corps responded that afternoon. While making a reconnaissance of the positions in front of the

105th Infantry on the afternoon of June 24, Ralph Smith saw a corps jeep approaching. A captain of the Adjutant General's staff dismounted and, after saluting, handed Smith a sealed envelope. Inside was a terse official corps order that stated that Major General Ralph Smith was relieved of command of the 27th Infantry Division of the United States Army. The letterhead of the order was that of the V Amphibious Corps, United States Marines.

Returning to the division command post, Smith was greeted by Major General Sanderford Jarman, who had been chosen by H. M. Smith to head the 27th Division. Jarman was an Army general with no recent combat experience. But H. M. Smith had wanted to sweep the command structure clean and the 27th mattered little to him, for he did not intend to use it ever again.

Ralph Smith was told by a member of the corps staff that his offer to remain and help Jarman get oriented was refused and that he was to leave the island immediately. He and one aide left before midnight on a plane that took them to Honolulu.

When then Army Ground Troop Commander Lieutenant General Robert Richardson learned of the relief of Smith and the appointment of Jarman, he acted quickly. On June 28, Richardson relieved Jarman of command of the 27th and replaced him with General George Griner, Commander of the 98th Infantry Division. He also assigned Ralph Smith to command the 98th. The tenure of Ralph Smith in the 98th was short, however, for Washington decided that it would be the better part of valor to remove Smith entirely from the theater where H. M. Smith was. He was soon posted to command the Infantry Replacement Training Center (IRTC) in Fort Robinson, Arkansas. But this posting was also short-lived, for Eisenhower was seeking a general officer fluent in French and adept in French customs. Ralph Smith, who had studied at the Sorbonne and lived in France on assignment, was the very person to become the newly appointed Military Attaché to the French government in Paris. And there he went.

Almost as if it were awaiting him, the Battle of the Bulge was taking place when Ralph Smith arrived in Paris to take up his position. The German offensive threatened Antwerp and disrupted the planned drive by the Allies to push on into Germany. Hard on the heels of the Bulge, the Germans attacked at the south end of the line, just at the juncture between the American 7th Army and the French 1st Army. They developed a salient that came to be known as the Colmar Pocket. Their pressure was great, and Lieutenant General Jacob Devers (Commander of the 6th Army Group, which included both the 1st French and the 7th American) decided that in order to correct the incursion into Allied lines, it would be advisable to withdraw from Strasbourg. This city was held in special regard by the French, and the thought of withdrawing from it and allowing it to return to German hands was just too much for the Free French Leader General Charles de Gaulle. In his regal manner, de Gaulle stated that if the Allies — the Americans — withdrew from Strasbourg without a fight, he would retaliate by closing French highways to American military vehicles. The issue suddenly became very sticky. The only supply line that the Americans and British had to their troops was over French highways. Diplomacy, rather than shouting, became the order of the day. Feverishly, American commanders and diplomats, including the U.S. Military Attaché in Paris, Ralph Smith, talked with the French and finally persuaded them that a fight would indeed be made to save Strasbourg. As it turned out, the Allies were able to hold Strasbourg and French honor was upheld. Ralph Smith, the quiet diplomat, played his part.

Once Saipan was taken and declared secure, the role of the fighting man on the island ended. H. M. Smith relinquished command of the V Amphibious Corps and took command of all Marine troops in the Pacific — but from behind a desk in Honolulu. As Marine units committed to combat came under the command of the Naval Task Force, Smith had little or no authority in governing Marines who were fighting, as was the case with General Richardson, who would have saved Ralph Smith if he could. While fuming in this desk job, H. M. Smith accepted an assignment from the *Saturday Evening Post* to write a series of articles explaining to the readers how and why he had fired Ralph Smith. The American public took up sides, and soon there was a mild brouhaha. The prestigious *Infantry Journal*, spokesmedium for the Army foot soldier, thought that H. M. Smith had acted precipitously.

An Army board, under Major General J. T. McNarney, convened and heard the evidence. It concluded that Ralph Smith had acted improperly in giving orders to the 105th Infantry (a part of the 27th Division, but at the time attached to V Corps) and in the unit's failure to advance as it should on June 23 and 24 in order to keep abreast of the Marine units on its flanks.

Learning from the bitter experience that had befallen the prideful U.S.

Army, General McNarney, Commander of the Army Ground Forces, publicly expressed serious doubt in the advisability of ever again placing Army units under the command of Lieutenant General Holland M. Smith.

Today Saipan is a tranquil tropical island. The Japanese airfield at its extreme north end is overgrown by recently sprouted trees. It is possible to walk among them, shaded from the sunlight. The ground is strewn with the residuals of war — unexploded shells, bayonets, and bits of discarded canteens, remnants of the fighting men who died there. In the stillness that is felt among those trees, it is almost possible to hear the rantings of Holland Smith and the quiet answers of Ralph Smith.

Epilogue to Saipan

On July 9, 1944, the day after H. M. Smith finally had his wish and replaced Ralph Smith as Commander of the 27th Infantry Division, Admiral Richmond Kelly Turner declared the island of Saipan secure. Officially, there was no longer Japanese resistance on the island and natives and Americans could move anywhere unmolested.

Among the troops that had come to Saipan in the last Japanese reinforcement was Captain Sakae Oba, an infantryman who was a reinforcement from a post with an infantry division fighting in China. While on a transport bound for the island, his ship was torpedoed by the Americans, and he spent some unhappy hours in the water before being rescued by Japanese patrol boats. When he arrived in Saipan, he was no longer wet and tired, but dry and rested. He still carried his sidearm and sword, which were both bright and shiny — ready to be used in duty to the Emperor.

Oba was posted to a front-line unit and fought during the slow grind that would eventually end the Japanese mandate on the island. Somehow, he found himself and a few of his command cut off from the battle and lodged on Mt. Tapotchau in the dense jungle. He decided that the battle had passed him and his followers. He determined to assemble as many as possible, retreat to the mountain, and await that time when Japan would again send reinforcements or, better still, an invasion force to retake the island.

And so he did! Over the following months, he made a camp, assembled more than 50 soldiers and an attached 150 Japanese civilians, and set about to survive, awaiting that day when the Emperor would return to victory.

In the infrequent brushes that his men had with American soldiers, they merely defended themselves, shunning the many, many times that they could have ambushed the Americans. They did this not out of compassion, but from a belief that to remain intact would be their only chance of keeping themselves as a cohesive fighting force ready to fulfill their mission when the Japanese returned.

The Americans soon knew that Oba and his men were out there, and they began to launch reconnaissance efforts to locate them. They then made company-sized attacks followed by several battalions, and, in their final effort, 5,000 Marines, almost shoulder-to-shoulder, swept the location where Oba was known to be. Oba had his men, *and civilians*, position themselves on precipitous ledges and in treetops, for, as they knew, Marines never look up — only ahead. Oba and his command escaped this search with but three casualties.

On went this cat-and-mouse game until, one day, the Americans began acting differently. Word came to Oba that the war had ended and the Emperor had ordered that all Japanese troops lay down their arms and surrender to the Americans. Entreaty to Oba was to no avail. He asked for proof. Finally, after several parties of Oba's command had actually met with the Americans, and after, at his insistence, Oba had received a written and chopped order from the Japanese General, Oba communicated that he would bring in his troops.

The evening before the fateful day, Oba had his command wash and prepare their uniforms. In the brilliant sunlight of December 1, 1945, Oba assembled his command and marched them from the mountain down to a clearing where the Americans awaited. As a final gesture to the Emperor, before leaving the camp, Oba ordered a full salute of all functioning arms. This was for Japan! He then slowly lowered, for the last time, the Rising Sun of Japan. When he reached the awaiting Americans, they, having heard the gunfire of the mountain, were doubtful about a peaceful surrender. When the command arrived, without flinching at the drawn American guns, Oba marched his troops into position. He ordered them to attention, had them lay down their arms, and then, and only then, did he walk forward and present his pistol and sword, both still shiny, to the American Marine Major who accepted the surrender.

That evening, Oba and his two surviving officers were feted to a dinner at the Marine Officers Club by all the Marine officers who could possibly attend.

Chapter 8

Bohn Speaks
Up at Normandy

*J**OHN J. BOHN** was born in St. Paul, Minnesota, in 1889. He enlisted in the Army in 1914 and served as private and sergeant until 1916 when he was commissioned second lieutenant, U.S. Cavalry, and promoted to first lieutenant on the same day. He served in the Philippines with a military survey party and in Mexico against Pancho Villa and received the Silver Star for his action at Guerrero in March*

1916. After being commissioned, he attended the Army Service School and then joined the 6th Cavalry in Texas. During World War I he was in France with the 6th and returned with the unit to Fort Oglethorpe, Georgia. In 1920-1921, he attended the Cavalry School, Fort Riley, Kansas. He served with the 12th Cavalry in Texas until 1921 when he was assigned to the Alabama National Guard. He returned to the Cavalry School in 1928 for the advanced course, then attended the Command and General Staff School at Fort Leavenworth, Kansas, in 1929, and served with the 7th Cavalry in Texas in 1931. He was graduated from the Army War College at Carlisle Barracks, Pennsylvania, in 1932, and after a tour with the Office of Chief of Cavalry and a tour with the Cavalry School he became executive officer of the school in 1939. He was assigned as Trains Commander of the 3rd Armored Division, Camp Polk, Louisiana, in 1941, was on temporary duty at the Armored Force School in 1941, and became Chief of Staff of the II Armored Corps, Camp Polk, Louisiana, in 1942. He was Commander of a combat command of the 3rd Armored Division and a brigadier general in 1942, which command he was holding at the time of the Normandy invasion when he was relieved of command, demoted to the rank of colonel, and returned to the States. He retired at this rank.

On March 1, 1942, the War Department reorganized the U.S. Armored Division from a triangular unit (containing three infantry regiments) to one containing "combat commands," not unlike "task forces" common to the Infantry Division — units of varying sizes but retaining a continuing command structure, forced and ordered to attain certain objectives within the scope of the Armored Division.

In a typical armored division were two armored regiments and one armored infantry regiment. Three armored artillery battalions supported the armor/infantry, each armed with self-propelled 105-mm howitzers. An armored reconnaissance battalion and an armored engineer battalion rounded out the assigned combat forces, while support forces that were assigned were an armored maintenance battalion, an armored supply battalion, an armored medical battalion, a signal company, a military police company, and the Division Headquarters Company. Frequently, there were attached

Then-Major John J. Bohn, January 1933, later to be relieved of command of Combat Command B, 3rd Armored Division. (Harris & Ewing, Washington, D.C./National Archives)

to an armored division such specialized units as a tank destroyer battalion and an anti-aircraft artillery battalion.

In the beginning of trial by fire of the new Table of Organization and Equipment (TO/E), it was recognized that if there were to be three relatively equal combat commands, it would be necessary to assign another armored infantry regiment to the division or to attach one. After this was done, the typical combat command had the following:

> one tank regiment, less one battalion
> one armored infantry regiment, less one battalion
> one artillery battalion
> one anti-aircraft battalion
> one engineer company
> one tank destroyer company
> one medical company
> one maintenance company

Although the division artillery officer in the infantry division was a brigadier general, he was but a colonel in the armored division, probably because his battalions were almost always attached to combat commands and seldom did they execute division-coordinated fire. The Division Commander was usually a major general and his assistant a brigadier general. Combat Commands A and B were commanded by brigadier generals, while the reserve combat command was commanded by a line colonel. The role, missions, and organization of the division reserve evolved, as did assigned strength, so that reserve came to be of equal strength to the principal Combat Commands A and B. The command of the reserve, however, was entrusted to a bird (full) colonel. But on occasion, the Assistant Division Commander, a brigadier general, commanded.

When combat commands were attached to neighboring units for the purpose of executing some special mission, as in exploiting a breakthrough, the attached element of an armored division operated much as any orphan unit, like an attached engineer battalion or a tank destroyer battalion — that is, the attached unit Commander never knew from one minute to the next what mission the Commander to whom he was attached would think of for him to try to do. There were instances during World War II in Europe when engineers were called to fight as infantry, and artillery was broken up into rifle squads to augment rifle companies.

From l to r: An unidentified Commander of the 33rd Armored Regiment, an unidentified British observer, and Brigadier General John J. Bohn, Commanding General of Combat Command B, 3rd Armored Division. (U.S. Army Signal Corps)

The attached combat command was especially vulnerable because it was at the mercy of peers and superiors who had little understanding of the capabilities and limitations of armored units and little respect for them. If the armored soldier can be thought of as playing the more skilled "wishbone" or "T" offense, the foot soldier could be considered to play from a simpler, single wing — "three yards in a cloud of dust" — comparable to brute force.

Within the armored division, and subordinate to the combat command, were task forces formed for a specific purpose — to secure a terrain feature or a bridge at such distance from the line of attack that foot soldiers could not reasonably be expected to reach it, yet close enough so that foot soldiers could get to the newly won objective and defend it against enemy counterattack (for armor is not the ideal defensive arm). The typical task force was comprised of:

> one tank battalion
> one infantry battalion, less one company
> one platoon of engineers
> one platoon of tank destroyers

A further subdivision was the battle group, which could be formed by a task force commander for the purpose of performing something like a "clean-up" job. Though the composition of the battle group varied, it could include units such as these:

> one infantry company
> one tank or tank-destroyer platoon
> one mortar platoon
> one engineer squad

The 3rd U.S. Armored Division wore the shoulder patch emblazoned with equal geometric figures of yellow (cavalry), blue (infantry), and red (artillery), with a cannon tube, track symbol, and red lightning bolt superimposed on the badge. Below the triangular patch was the word "SPEARHEAD," the name by which the division wished to be known. Its first Commander was Brigadier General Alvan C. Gillem, a Suwanee (University of the South) graduate who later commanded the II Corps stateside and the Desert Training Center before going to Europe to command a corps. When he left the 3rd, he took with him to II Corps Colonel John J. Bohn as Chief of Staff. Sensing the opportunity for a promotion for an especially good officer, Gillem sent Bohn back to the 3rd to command one of the combat commands and to become a brigadier general.

The cadre for the yet-to-be-formed 3rd Armored Division came from the 2nd Armored, stationed at Camp Polk, Louisiana. They arrived at Camp Beauregard, Louisiana, in April 1941 to activate the division. Their training was uneventful, but included a stint at the Desert Training Center in the Mojave Desert. Upon completion of training in Louisiana, the division departed for England. When Gillem left to command the II Corps, he

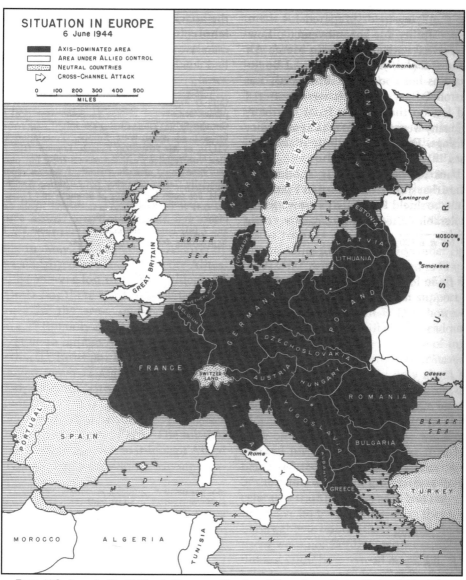

From *U.S. Army in World War II: European Theater of Operations, Cross-Channel Attack*, by Gordon A. Harrison (Washington, D.C.: U.S. Army, Office of the Chief of Military History, 1951), 268.

was replaced by Major General Walton Walker, himself destined to notoriety. He left the 3rd in August 1942 to command the newly formed IV Armored Corps. Brigadier General Leroy H. Watson, who had been in charge

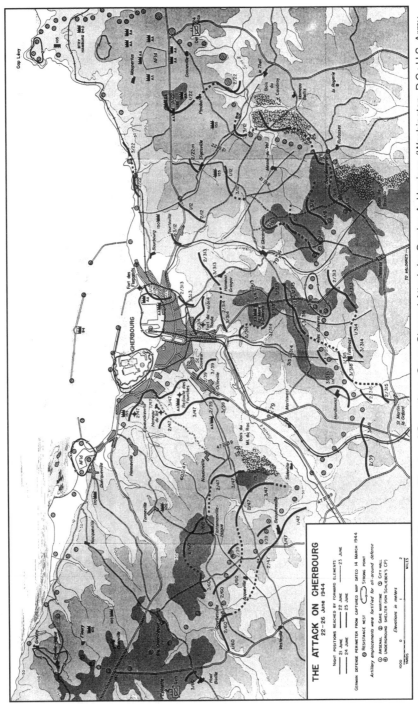

THE ATTACK ON CHERBOURG
22–26 June 1944

NIGHT POSITIONS REACHED BY FORWARD ELEMENTS
——— 21 JUNE   ——— 22 JUNE   ——— 23 JUNE
——— 24 JUNE   ——— 25 JUNE

GERMAN DEFENSE PERIMETER FROM CAPTURED MAP DATED 14 MARCH 1944
✹ RESISTANCE NEST   ⌢ STRONG POINT

Artillery emplacements were fortified for all-around defense
Ⓐ ARSENAL   Ⓑ GARE MARITIME   Ⓔ CITY HALL
Ⓒ UNDERGROUND SHELTER (VON SCHLIEBEN'S CP)

Elevations in meters

From *U.S. Army in World War II: European Theater of Operations, Cross-Channel Attack*, by Gordon A. Harrison (Washington, D.C.: U.S. Army, Office of the Chief of Military History, 1951), Map XXIV.

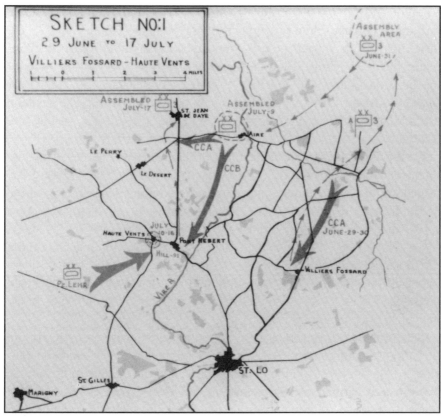

Attack of Combat Command B, 3rd Armored Division, from the division operations maps and *Spearhead in the West: History of the 3rd Armored Division.* (Military Press, 1946)

of one of the combat commands, assumed command of the division. It was at this time that Bohn was promoted to brigadier general and given command of Combat Command B.

The division completed maneuvers in September/October 1942 and then was railed to Camp Pickett, Virginia, and then to Indiantown Gap, Pennsylvania. In the summer of 1943, the division shipped out to Camp Kilmer, New Jersey, and sailed for England, where it arrived in mid-September 1943. It was stationed in Wiltshire where it intensified gunnery training under officers recently returned from actual battlefield experience.

Early in June 1944, the 3rd made ready (as did others) to sail the English Channel to Normandy. It arrived at the ports of embarkation, Southhampton and Weymouth, on June 18 and 19, 1944, and set sail on the 23rd, arriving at Omaha White (a segment of Omaha Beach) on that day. As the beach had by then been secured, the division was able to move unimpeded inland to Isigny. Though it took until July 4 to get all the units of the division ashore and together, the area Commander, General Omar Bradley, lost no time in putting the new arrivals to work. The division assembled some five miles northeast of the village of Vire, on the Vire River.

At the time, there existed in the German defense line a salient that threatened the opposing U.S. 29th Infantry Division. The U.S. 3rd Armored, on the 29th's flank, opposed the German Fusilier Battalion of the 353rd Infantry Division. This German Wehrmacht Division was comprised of the 941st, 942nd, and 943rd Grenadier Regiments, 353rd Artillery Regiment, 353rd Fusilier Battalion, 353rd Anti-tank Battalion, 353rd Engineer Battalion, and 353rd Signal Battalion. The Germans were in a well-prepared position and supported by their division artillery and anti-tank forces. They were also well entrenched behind the fabled hedgerows of Normandy.

Seeing the predicament that the Allied attackers were about to face in their first taste of combat, XIX Corps issued the newly invented and constructed "tank-dozers" to the command and told the tankers to breach the tree-covered earthen obstacles that lay between each field as a terrain fence to separate a farmer from his neighbor. Since the first dividing of ground into tilled fields centuries before, the fields, as they were plowed, were separated from one another by unplowed rows, which had accumulated a number of trees and a thick thorny bramble growth, so thick that no man could pass through. Also, as the centuries passed, the plowing diminished the general ground elevation in the tilled fields while it elevated the hedgerows.

For the attack on the German 353rd, which was to take place on the morning of June 29, Brigadier General Doyle Hicky, Commander of Combat Command A of the 3rd Armored, divided his command into two task forces, X and Y, under the command of Colonel T. E. Boudinot and a Colonel Parks, with the reserve task force, TFZ, commanded by a Lieutenant Colonel Abney, the support trains by a Lieutenant Colonel Brown, and the artillery support coming from the 54th Field Artillery Battalion and the general support of the 391st and 967th Field Artillery Battalions. As was customary, the 32nd Armored Regiment fought

Combat Command B, 3rd Armored Division, en route to Pont Ebert. (The sign was in German.) (U.S. Army Signal Corps)

Combat Command B, 3rd Armored Division, passing through the village of Airel. (U.S. Army Signal Corps)

Dismounted troops of Combat Command B, 3rd Armored Division, at Haute Vents. (U.S. Army Signal Corps)

under Combat Command A, while the 33rd fought under Combat Command B.

When the attack was launched with Task Force X on the left and Task Force Y on the right, it followed a short but intense artillery barrage. TFX soon reached the woods at La Forge-Bois de Bretel by noon and, having achieved the objective assigned by the combat command commander, was told to halt and dig in. Less rapid was the advance of the other task force, which slugged along until, in the late afternoon, it reached its objective — the little stream north of Villiers-Fossard. At these locations, the task

A column of Combat Command B, 3rd Armored Division, awaiting order to attack. (U.S. Army Signal Corps)

forces paused for the night and then resumed the attack on the morning of June 30, which they continued until the combat command objective was overrun at about noon. There the two task forces dug in and waited the next assignment.

In the short but spirited action of Combat Command A, the losses numbered 31 tanks destroyed, 12 other vehicles destroyed, and 451 men killed or wounded. It was a costly beginning for the young division.

Meanwhile, Combat Command B, under Brigadier General John J. Bohn, was assigned to the 30th Infantry Division and immediately given the task by the 30th to exploit a shallow and narrow bridgehead that had been secured over the Vire River at Airel. In front of the bridgehead was the fabled Panzer Lehr Division.

The exposed surface of the plain at Normandy was gently undulating, though principally flat, and drainage was primarily toward the coast and tending north at the location where the 3rd Armored Division took its place. Streams, while in no sense presenting a major transportation artery, were nevertheless sufficiently deep and wide to become terrain obstacles, except at the location of bridges. Hence, there was the necessity to secure bridges, intact, if possible.

The days up to July 9 were spent by the men of Combat Command B moving into the positions of attack at the shallow bridgehead at Airel. The movement into the line of attack was made under heavy artillery from the enemy. The objective of Combat Command B was to attack south toward St. Giles, through Pont Hebert and Haute Vents.

It just so happened that at the time Combat Command B was receiving orders from the 30th to attack south, their opponent, the Panzer Lehr Division, was receiving orders to retake Isigny. Something akin to a meeting engagement was in the making.

The Panzer Lehr had been formed of demonstration units of the Panzer Training School at Potsdam and also from the Bergin Maneuver Area of Wehrkreis (defense sector) XI. These units had been selected because they had been teaching the doctrine of repelling tank and infantry attack and were considered the most likely to form a "super division." Shortly after its organization in the early part of 1944, the Panzer Lehr acquired the 901st Infantry Lehr Regiment from its previous station in and around Budapest. When the division arrived at the Normandy front in the late spring of 1944, it had 110 Tiger tanks, 40 tracked assault guns, and more than 600 tracked and half-tracked vehicles. This complement of armor made the division the strongest in the German army, though it had not seen combat; it was not gun-shy, but experienced only in theory.

The Lehr — comprised of the 130th Panzer Regiment, 901st and 902nd Panzer Grenadier Regiments, 130th Panzer Artillery Regiment, 130th Panzer Reconnaissance Battalion, 130th Panzer Anti-tank Battalion, 130th Panzer Engineer Battalion, 130th Panzer Signal Battalion, and 311th Army Anti-aircraft Battalion — was commanded by Lieutenant General Fritz Bayerling, who had been an enlisted man in World War I. After he was demobilized at that war's end, he was unable to find employment but he was able to persuade the board before which he appeared that he was of unique worth to the new army of the Weimar Republic. Henceforth, he received a direct commission, and even in the General Staff. By 1941, he had risen to the rank of brigadier general and was posted to Field Marshal Erwin Rommel's Afrika Korps as Chief of Staff in 1942, and then Chief of Staff of the Panzer Army Afrika later in the year. He was appointed Acting Commander of the Afrika Korps in 1942 and became Chief of Staff of the 1st German-Italian Panzer Army as it fought in Tunisia. Before Tunis, in the last struggle to hold out, he was wounded and evacuated to Europe. Upon his recovery, he commanded the 3rd Panzer Division in Russia in 1943, before being given the command of the Lehr.

The U.S. 3rd Armored Division's Brigadier General John J. Bohn was a solidly built man — not fat, but solid — and rather short for his build. He had a square face and was determined in his demeanor. He had served several distinguished soldiers well as their Chief of Staff before taking command of Combat Command B of the 3rd Armored. When the order came attaching Combat Command B to the 30th Infantry Division, General Bohn was too new to the game to know what this meant to those being attached. He had seen attachment before only as a senior staff officer, not as the affected Commander. In Army language, attachment simply meant that he would take orders from the Commanding General of the division to which he was attached, just as he would from his own Division Commander, Major General Leroy Watson. Attaching a combat command or a task force from an armored division was not unlikely, and tankers had come to expect to be attached sometime during their combat careers. But tanks were frequently misused by the infantry, who expected them to be a secret super weapon that would annihilate the enemy.

If Bohn were called to issue forth his tanks laden with infantrymen hanging all over them, this he would do. If he were called to carry ammunition and C rations to foxholes and to remove the wounded and dead, this he would do. If he were called to dismount and fight as infantry, this he would do. In short, he would use his armored, cannon-bearing tanks exactly as the infantry told him to do.

Obeying his orders, General Bohn hastily made for the front along with his Operations officer so that he might meet and get to know his new Commander and also to learn the mission that he was certain he was to be given. It was one of those blissful, balmy July days when Bohn arrived at the farmhouse in Isigny where the division command post of the 30th was located. It was easy to find the location of the command post, for the division had displayed an ample number of signs bearing the oval red and blue insignia of the Old Hickory Division, raised in Tennessee and named for Andrew Jackson. General Bohn entered the stone building and was immediately brought to the room occupied by the Commander of the 30th Division, Major General Leland S. Hobbs, and (to the surprise of Bohn) the Commander of the XIX Corps, Major General Charles H. "Cowboy Pete" Corlett.

Leland Hobbs was, by association with General Omar Bradley, untouchable. General Bradley wrote in *A General's Story*:

> Leland Hobbs was a classmate and close friend. . . . At West Point he had a big strong jaw and a stubborn streak a mile wide . . . His division was a perfect expression of his character. Hobbs was a hard charger.

According to Bradley, early in the attack Hobbs took his division across the Vire and gained a significant bridgehead. The men attempted "to exploit" the bridgehead with parts of Leroy Watson's 3rd Armored Division, which was led by the Assistant Commander, John J. Bohn, "but the area was too confined." The men met "fierce enemy resistance, and as a consequence the XIX Corps attack likewise failed to punch the crust." So much for Bradley's impartiality as far as Hobbs was concerned.

Then there was "Cowboy Pete" Corlett. He had been with the 7th Hourglass Division on the island of Attu in the Aleutians when Major General Albert E. Brown was sacked. Corlett had witnessed injustice to Brown, and now he was about to deal out a bit himself. In Attu, with the departure of Major General Eugene Landrum (who had replaced the sacked Brown), Corlett had assumed command of the 7th Division and had taken it to Kwajalein, where he fought the island war with such aplomb that, after it was all over, he became one of the few senior Commanders who left the Pacific to go to the European Theater of Operations. He did so with a promotion from brigadier to major general and an increase in responsibility, for in Europe he commanded a corps.

Generals Bohn, Hobbs, and Corlett exchanged pleasantries, which were followed by a situation briefing from the Operations officer (G-3) of the 30th. To a tanker such as Bohn, the situation was far from favorable for the use of armor to break German resistance and to counter the impending

The village of Airel after the shelling of 3rd Armored Division artillery and the corps artillery. (U.S. Army Signal Corps)

thrust of the Lehr Division, which was expected to hit almost simultaneously with the planned breakthrough of American armor.

The village of Airel, with a thousand inhabitants, was typical of rural Normandy towns, with stone and mortar buildings enclosing wood frames that, in turn, supported wood-beamed tile roofs. The buildings afforded good protection from ground burst (laterally dispersed shrapnel), but provided only minimal protection from air bursts. In an artillery barrage, the building's cellar afforded almost complete protection. As with most rural European villages, the streets were wide, allowing good access or turnaround and retreat for vehicles, unless the streets were filled with stone rubble resulting from intense artillery bombardment. Beside and through the eastern extremity of the village, and running north-south, was the Vire River. At the village, the river was no more than 70 yards wide, but it was swift and its sandy banks were vertical. The river was spanned by a multiple-arched stone bridge, barely wide enough to allow passage of a Sherman tank, and only wide enough to allow passage of a tank-dozer if it was to cross with the blade raised, which hindered the forward sight of the tank driver. But numerous vehicles, including tank-dozers, of the 30th Division used the bridge continuously, and the division engineer had reported the bridge safe for passage.

The valued bridgehead that the 30th had secured over the Vire included the village and extended a few hundred yards beyond into the farmland to the west. It was this bridgehead that the tanks of the 30th were called to "exploit," but this mission was being resisted by what was reported by the division G-2 (Intelligence) to be infantry, lightly supported by armor, tenaciously entrenched and sufficiently strong to stop and repulse the several attacks that had been launched by the battalions of the 30th. And, as Intelligence reported, the situation was critical, for the Panzer Lehr Division might attack at any moment and even erase the tenuous hold on the bridgehead. What was not known by American Intelligence was that even at the moment of the briefing, the Lehr was approaching the line of departure for an attack that had as its objective nothing so limited as erasing the bridgehead but rather the port of Isigny.

The plan of attack that Operations (G-3) of the 3rd Armored Division gave to General Bohn on June 30 called on his Combat Command B of the 3rd Armored Division to cross the bridge into Airel and charge out of the village into the farmland to the west. The advance was to go as far and as fast as resistance would allow. A primary objective was the village of Haute Vents, some ten miles to the south.

General Bohn's appraisal of the situation led him to the conclusion that he was being asked to lead his tanks into an unprotected thrust that could easily catch them with unguarded flanks in the midst of a formidable German counterattack by the Lehr Division, which might even launch an attack against the bridgehead. What if they were to get out of the town, go miles into German territory, and, out there exposed, have the Lehr Division hit their only avenue of retreat (the bridge), retake it, or, worse still, destroy it? They would be cut off, without gasoline supply, without covering infantry, without a ghost of a chance against a whole division of German armor. Boldness is a tanker's forte, but foolishness is not. Bohn could see no way to do what was being asked of him without encountering the certainty of a German armored counterthrust.

When it came time in the meeting of the generals for Bohn to speak to the proposed plan, he stated what was on his mind and concluded with the suggestion of a more modest thrust with a task force of tanks having the objective of dislodging the Germans from their stranglehold on the bridgehead. Bohn stated his case calmly, but at the close of his argument, against the recommendation for a shallow attack to dislodge the defenders, he had the temerity to give Major Generals Hobbs and Corlett a short lecture on the proper use of armor by the infantry.

Bohn was interrupted by General Hobbs before he could finish the tactical lesson. Hobbs almost shouted that his infantrymen had been holding back enemy counterattacks for two days and had in the process taken unnecessarily high casualties. The more that Hobbs talked, the more his temper rose and the louder his voice grew. He ended with the accusation that the tankers were unwilling to fight. This brought a sharp retort from Bohn, who said again that the armor was being asked to do something that it was not suited for and something that the infantry was incapable of doing.

Corlett, who had remained silent, then entered the argument — of course, on the side of Hobbs — already mad. He affirmed and supported the sensibility of Hobbs's plan, and he, too, questioned Bohn's willingness to fight. Bohn retorted to this and soon both Corlett and Hobbs were shouting at Bohn, who in return was shouting back. Corlett finally ended the argument by angrily demanding Bohn to commence the attack as he had been ordered.

Bohn left the meeting with Hobbs and Corlett furious, yet he would follow their orders no matter what the consequences. He began to assemble the combat command to launch the attack that would take place the next dawn, July 1. Tanks and half-tracks moved into position while the attack orders were being issued. Under the cover of a moonlit night, the preparations continued almost until the time for the jump-off.

Hobbs and Corlett had not been idle. They made contact with Omar Bradley at Army Headquarters and received his blessing to relieve Bohn for the miscalculation of stating his mind to two major generals. In typical fashion, Bradley believed that it would be a waste of time to bother hearing Bohn's side of the story. Yet, because Bohn had left the conference fully ready to carry out Hobbs's and Corlett's orders, it must be concluded that their decision to relieve him was because he had the gall to tell them that they were ordering an improper use of tanks, and in a situation that was far from being desperate. Unfortunately, time was to prove Bohn to have been correct in every detail.

Just before dawn, when the attack was to take place, Hobbs sent for Bohn and ordered him to report to the division command post. Bohn protested the order, for it meant that he had to travel ten miles in blackout and against the flow of armor up to the front for the attack. Furthermore,

Bohn believed that his place was in the command tank directing the attack, which was to take place in but a few hours. But he was told to go as directed. When he arrived, a blustering Hobbs told Bohn of his transgressions and ended the tirade by stating that Bohn was incapable of following orders he didn't believe would result in success. Hobbs told Bohn that he was relieved of command and that he would turn over his former command to T. E. Boudinot, who was even then on his way to assume the new assignment. Bohn heard him out, then returned to where the command was making ready for the attack. He called battalion and company Commanders on the radio and told them of the relief and the name of the new Commander and wished them well in the attack. It came as a blow to these tankers, artillerymen, medics, tank destroyers, and engineers to learn that the quarterback that they had practiced with was benched and a new, unknown quarterback would be calling signals.

While Bohn was radioing his good-byes, his replacement appeared. Together they surveyed the situation. When the newly arrived Commander was familiar with the situation and the battle orders from Hobbs, Bohn volunteered to stay around to help. His successor would have welcomed him, but he had been ordered by Hobbs and Corlett to have Bohn quit the field, get in his jeep, and return to 3rd Armored Division Headquarters. Bohn did as he was told and rode away, leaving his aide to pack his belongings and follow.

The attack jumped off as scheduled. Tanks rumbled across the Vire River and through the village of Airel, which was filled with watchful infantrymen. The artillery blazed away and the earth shook in the farmlands to the west where the shells were falling. Almost as in answer, the Germans began a barrage themselves, which began to pulverize the village of Airel. The advancing tanks had to pick their way through the mounting rubble. The village bridge, the only one for ten miles in either direction on the river, received some damage from surface bursts, but it soon became apparent that the Germans were not intent on destroying the bridge. Had they wished, they could have done so; but they intended to use it in their attack plans. As the American tanks emerged from the village into the farmlands, the approaching tanks of the Lehr Division appeared. The battle of fire and maneuver had begun.

And thus developed one of the most intense tank-versus-tank battles of the Normandy campaign. In the slowly brightening dawn, tankers on both sides began to zero in on targets. The American tanks managed to dislodge the infantry frontline German defenders and, having roared over their emplacements, kept on moving — but toward German Tiger tanks that were quite different in killing power from the displaced German infantry. Had there been places in the battle terrain that would furnish cover or concealment, the battle might have been different. But with both sides exposed, it was simply a matter of fire and maneuver and kill or be killed. Slowly, it became apparent to the Allied tankers that the Germans possessed superior armor and superior numbers in armor and that they were intent not only on annihilating the Americans but also on driving them through the village, up the road to Isigny, and back into the Channel. This was not merely a counterattack, it was an attack in force, and the American armor was but an irritant, not a deterrent.

One of the attacking Commanders of the lead tank companies was the first to order a retreat into the shelter of the village. As the armor made its way back into Airel, the Germans began to concentrate their direct fire on the visible entrance into the village. Disabled vehicles, incapacitated in the advance, impeded the withdrawal. In the confusion, additional vehicles were incapacitated, adding further to the difficulty of withdrawal by mobile but retreating American armor. Some of the American armor had not been ordered to retreat and held their ground providing covering fire. Many of these rear-guard vehicles were destroyed at the place of their farthest advance.

The German Lehr slowly pushed its way across the open fields and made for the village. At noon, the Germans had either disabled or driven back all the American attackers. What had begun as a hopeful, spirited assault had turned into a desperate defense of Airel by the combined American infantry and armor. Luckily for the Americans, the Germans found it difficult to attack them inside the village. In the late afternoon, the German armor broke off the strike and retreated beyond the range of direct antitank fire.

In front of the village, in its streets, and in the fields beyond where the battle had raged, the landscape was littered with German and American vehicles that would fight no more. The Americans lost more than 40 halftracks and wheeled vehicles and suffered more than 400 casualties. For Combat Command B of the 3rd Armored Division, its first taste of battle had indeed been a costly learning experience. But it was destined to go on under Boudinot (soon to be a brigadier general). When the unit arrived in open country, about a month later, it did show the willingness and capability and gained the accomplishments that were expected of armor, for it was then operating under favorable circumstances.

In the meantime, Brigadier General John Bohn returned to the 3rd Armored Division command post to receive two rude and bitter surprises. Orders were waiting that reduced him from brigadier general to the rank of colonel and transferred him from France back through England to America for reassignment. He had suffered the most severe punishment any relieved commander received during the entire war. And all of this misfortune came to him for stating (or shouting) a prediction of the outcome of an attack to which he had objected. Ironically, he returned to America to a training assignment teaching the doctrine of tank deployment.

Hobbs went on with his Old Hickory Division to mount a distinguished record across France and into Germany, but Corlett was not so lucky. He chose to "mouth off" to Courtney Hodges (the Army Commander) at a later time and was himself relieved.

Chapter 9

Landrum,
the "Tough Ombre"

E UGENE M. LANDRUM *was born in Pensacola, Florida, in 1891, enlisted in the Army in 1910, and served as a private and sergeant in the coast artillery and infantry until he accepted a commission as a second lieutenant, U.S. Infantry, in the fall of 1916. Having served in Florida, Georgia, Texas, and Hawaii before being commissioned, at that occasion he was assigned to the 32nd Infantry in Hawaii and in the Philippines*

until the end of World War I, when he joined the American Ex-
peditionary Force in Siberia. In 1919 he was posted at the Gen-
eral Service Schools in Kansas, from whence he became the of-
ficer in charge of the Correspondence Division of the Adjutant
General Department. In 1924, he transferred from U.S. Infantry
to Adjutant General. For several years he was with the 9th
Corps area at the Presidio in San Francisco.

A return to combat arms became a possibility when, in 1931,
Landrum matriculated at the Command and General Staff
School at Fort Leavenworth, Kansas. Upon graduation, as an
infantryman again, he became a Battalion Commander in the
6th Infantry at Jefferson Barracks, Missouri. With the regiment
he went to Illinois, and from there he was posted to duty with
the Civilian Conservation Corps until 1934, when he joined 6th
Corps Area Headquarters in Chicago in various staff positions.
He was graduated from the Army War College at Carlisle Bar-
racks, Pennsylvania, in 1936 and became an instructor at the
Infantry School, Fort Benning, Georgia, the same year, becom-
ing, in succession, secretary and executive officer. From there
he became a staff officer of the 3rd Infantry Division in Wash-
ington State. When he was assigned to the Alaskan Defense
Command in 1942, he became a brigadier general, 8th Infantry
Division, later replacing the former Commanding General, Al-
bert E. Brown, who was relieved just as he broke Japanese re-
sistance. A year later, when Landrum took command of the 87th
Infantry Division, he became a major general. For a short time
he was the Commanding General of the 71st Infantry Division,
and in 1944 he commanded the Infantry Replacement Training
Center at Camp Maxey, Texas. In the Normandy invasion, Lan-
drum took command of the poorly trained 90th Division and
held this dubious honor until he too was relieved. He returned
to stateside assignments and retired at his highest temporary
rank, major general.

At St.-Mihiel and in the Meuse-Argonne of World War I, the men of the
90th U.S. Infantry Division began calling themselves "Tough Ombres";
the nickname stuck when the division was reactivated at Camp Barkley,
Texas, in late March of 1942. The red $\overline{O}$ of the division patch stood for

Major General Eugene M. Landrum, appointed by "Lightning Joe" Collins to command the 90th Infantry Division (the "Tough Ombres"), which was described by Omar Bradley as, "the worst trained division to arrive in the European Theater of Operations." Landrum was relieved because he couldn't find a way for his troops to breach the hedgerows of Normandy. (90th Infantry Division Press, U.S. Army Signal Corps)

Texas-Oklahoma, from whence most of the World War I cadre had come. When reactivation occurred in World War II, however, men came from all over America, for the policy was to bring up to strength reactivated units that had only received a cadre of trained personnel who would form the nucleus of the unit-to-be. The 357th, 358th, and 359th Infantry Regiments; 343rd, 344th, and 915th Artillery Battalions (105-mm) and 345th Artillery Battalion (155-mm); 90th Signal Company; 415th Quartermaster Battalion; 90th Recon Troop; 315th Medical Battalion; and 315th Engineers were the assigned units of the newly formed 90th Division. Major General Henry Terrill commanded the division, and Brigadier General John E. Lewis commanded the artillery. Once basic training had been completed, a four-day inspection occurred by ranking Mexican officers, who found

From *U.S. Army in World War II: European Theater of Operations, Cross-Channel Attack* by Gordon A. Harrison (Washington, D.C.: U.S. Army, Office of the Chief of Military History, 1951), Map VII.

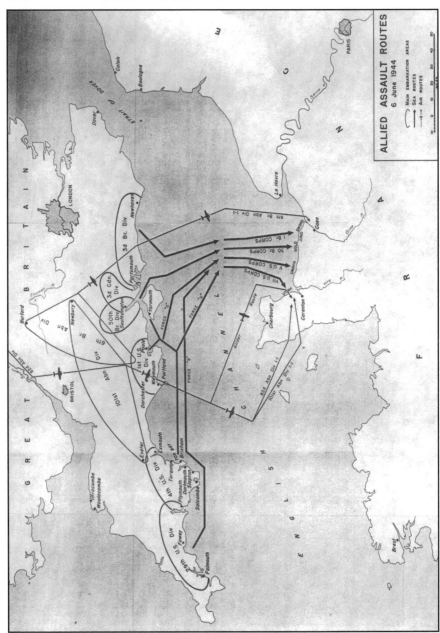

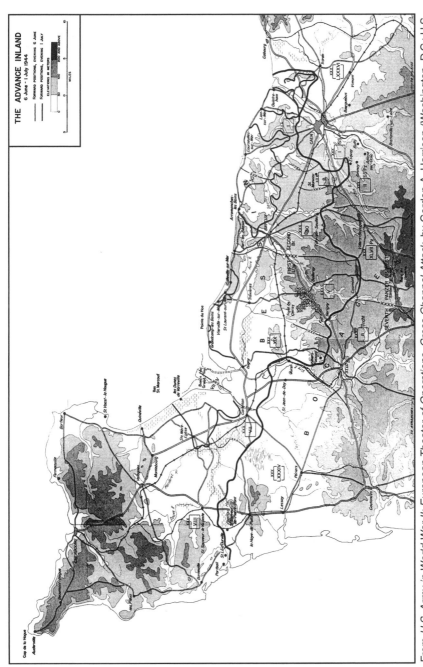

From *U.S. Army in World War II: European Theater of Operations, Cross-Channel Attack*, by Gordon A. Harrison (Washington, D.C.: U.S. Army, Office of the Chief of Military History, 1951), Map XXV.

the division typical of the newly reactivated organizations in the American Army and who had enthusiastic admiration for the military appearance of the unit. (This inspection was a rather bizarre ploy by the War Department to curry the favor of the Mexicans.)

Following such accolades, the 90th Division immediately joined the Louisiana maneuvers (war games in which large units fought imaginary battles and were judged by umpires) for two months, then returned to Camp Barkley for specialized training in close combat and attacks of fortified positions. A short stint in the desert followed, during late summer and early fall of 1943, and then the division headed to Fort Dix, New Jersey, to prepare for the staging from Camp Kilmer early in the year 1944. While awaiting embarkation from New York, Brigadier General Jay W. McKelvie assumed command. In March, the division sailed and arrived in England in early April. Except for two battalions of the 359th Infantry, which were the guests of the 4th Division in Devonshire, the remainder of the 90th was stationed in country camps north and east of Newport and Cardiff, in Wales. Sophisticated "state-of-the-art" training was received in mine detection, village fighting, hedgerow fighting, and survival techniques, which were intended to prepare the division for the fighting on the continent.

On D-Day, June 6, in midmorning, the two battalions of the 359th Infantry Regiment that had been with the 4th Division while in England were the first members of the 90th Division to set foot on the soil of France. Still attached to the 4th Division, these battalions of the "Tough Ombres" moved inland to St. Martin de Verreville.

The remainder of the 90th Division set sail for France on D-Day in four transports: the *Susan B. Anthony*, the *Excelsior*, the *Explorer*, and the *Beinville*. When these ships arrived the following morning, the *Susan B. Anthony*, carrying the division advance detachment and the remaining battalion of the 359th, promptly struck a mine. Though there was no loss of life as a result of the *Anthony*'s sinking, all equipment (except individual equipment) was lost, and it was some days before it could be replaced. The next day, June 8, the remainder of the division arrived at Utah Beach, and by nightfall all of the infantry of the division had been collected in several neighboring villages, and the division command was nearby.

The 90th was assigned to the VII Corps of the 1st Army. The first order the division received was to cross the Merderet River, attack westward, and seize the high ground east of the Douve River, 13 kilometers distant, in order to deepen the corps' beachhead. The division jumped off in the early morning hours of June 10 with the 357th and 358th Infantry Regiments in the attack. They crossed the Merderet in good order but stopped almost immediately, for the German defenders were entrenched behind the fabled hedgerows that brought so much grief in Normandy.

In front of the VII Corps, commanded by General James Lawton Collins, were the German 709th and 91st Infantry Divisions. The 709th was comprised of the 729th and 739th Infantry Regiments, 709th Artillery Battalion, 709th Engineer Battalion, and 709th Signal Company. It was formed as an understrength static division and was comprised of older men. It had been formed in Brittany, France, in the spring of 1941 and had remained there until 1943 when it had been transferred to Cherbourg to serve as the city's garrison. At that time, the division received the 919th Grenadier Regiment from the 242nd Infantry Division. Even with the addition of this fresh, young unit, the average age of the German division was 36. Lieutenant General Karl-Wilhelm von Schieben had previously led the 18th Panzer Division in the fall of 1943, when, while fighting against furious Russian attacks before Kiev, the division suffered such great losses that it was necessary to disband. It was from this bitter campaign that General von Schieben came to Normandy.

The German 91st Division was organized as an air landing division, but for all practical purposes it operated as a line infantry division. It was comprised of the 1057th and 1058th Grenadier Regiments, 91st Fusilier Company, 191st Anti-Tank Battalion, 191st Engineer Battalion, and 191st Signal Battalion. It was first commanded by Major General Wilhelm Falley, who gained a certain distinction when, on June 6, his Headquarters was attacked by paratroopers of the U.S. 82nd Airborne Division, and he became the first German general officer to be killed by American forces. It is thought that command of the division passed to Colonel Eugene Konig and that the decimated division had merged with the 77th Infantry Division.

The 77th Division had arrived in Normandy in the early winter of 1944 and was on the coast between the Contentin and Brittany peninsulas on D-Day. It was comprised of the 1049th and 1050th Grenadier Regiments, 177th Artillery Regiment, 177th Anti-Tank Battalion, 177th Engineer Battalion, 77th Fusilier Regiment, and 77th Signal Battalion. At the time of the invasion, the division was commanded by a Major General Stegmann.

Some of its units contained veterans of the 346th Infantry Division, which itself had received something of a mauling at the hands of the British during the Normandy invasion, but in the British sector.

Though hardly into the third day ashore and striving to reach the high ground east of the Douve River, the U.S. 90th Division was already in deep trouble. Though some of its trouble came from the Germans, most came from the American side. The Corps Commander, General J. Lawton Collins, and 1st Army's Commander at the time, Lieutenant General Courtney Hodges, began to sense that the training of the division had left much to be desired. Bradley wrote that the 90th "turned out to be one of the worst-trained divisions to arrive in the ETO." Major General Jay McKelvie, the Commanding General of the 90th, had grown up as a "red-legged" artilleryman — so named for the red-striped trousers the men wore — and was thought to be good at that, but never had he commanded infantry nor had he done more than furnish them fire support. When the 90th's attack mired down somewhere between the Douve and the Merderet Rivers, General Collins became disgusted and told Omar Bradley he wanted to make some changes. Bradley approved, though one of the two stepped in and saved McKelvie from disgrace. He was relieved "without prejudice" and sent to Italy. Two of his Regimental Commanders, from the 357th and 358th, were also relieved and sent to less demanding duties in England. Collins selected his very own Chief of Staff, Major General Eugene M. Landrum, to be the new Commander of the 90th. Gene Landrum was, like "Lightning Joe" Collins, a veteran of the very different war in the Pacific. But Collins had the utmost confidence that Landrum could and would turn the 90th into the division he wished it to be.

In order to understand the effect of the Normandy hedgerows on military tactics, one must imagine a gently undulating terrain cut by a few drainage courses and divided into agricultural parcels, some irregular in dimension and none very large, varying between several to 20 acres in area. Due to elevation, a hedgerow commanded the terrain surrounding it, save for similar hedgerows that were equal to but not greater than it. Because of vegetation, rows provided both cover and concealment. A defender could station himself behind a row, dig in, place outpost protection on the rows perpendicular to that which he intended to defend, and await the attack. When an attack came, the defender would be warned by outposts from their vantage along the rows in front. The outpost defenders could retreat under cover down the axis of a row until secure within the main defense position. Both automatic weapons and mortars could be employed to a greater advantage by the defender than by the attacker. Machine guns, situated at the flanks of a position, could cross-fire with each other and create a final firing line that was virtually impenetrable. Attackers were at disadvantage however they might try to strike. An assault along the axis of a row was not possible, for the surface impedance (the trees and brambles) was so dense that soldiers simply couldn't fight through. To strike across a field was almost as bad, for the attackers found the fields to be "killing fields." In contrast, if artillery and small-arms fire became so intense as to make a position untenable, the defenders had but to quit the row that they occupied and retreat to the one behind, there to assume a defense position as tenacious as the one just quit.

Interestingly, the tactical problems an attacker might face in fighting across country traversed by hedgerows was considered while the Allies were yet in England, and it had been concluded that it would be dealt with when it came up. But the presence of hedgerows in the Normandy terrain did exacerbate an age-old military principle: One is judged by how well one keeps up with one's neighbors on the right and on the left. Lag behind and you're not fighting hard enough; get out too far in front and you're not protecting your flanks and you're endangering the whole process by grandstanding.

Collins had a strong corps comprised of the 4th Infantry Division commanded by Major General Barton, the 9th Infantry Division commanded by Major General Manton Eddy, the 72nd Airborne commanded by Major General Matthew Ridgway, and the 90th Infantry Division. It was usually the practice of tactical Commanders who were fortunate to have four or even three units at their disposal to retain one as a reserve so that enemy weaknesses, disclosed during the initial assault, could be exploited by bringing in the reserve so that victory might be assured. But there also remained the question the Commander had to ask himself, "Do I use my best or poorest as reserve?" And the corollary to this question was, "Should I compare the performance of my best with that of my worst?" These questions were important to both Collins and Bradley at this particular time, for the 90th had already been branded as the most poorly trained of any division to arrive in the theater. Keep in mind that Landrum, the 90th's new Commander, was the choice of Collins, not of Bradley, so one might be sure that Bradley, intent on installing his own man, would be watching for any excuse to sack yet another and make his own selection. As fate would have it, the occasion was not long in coming.

The VII Corps was assigned the task of wresting the Cotentin peninsula and the port of Cherbourg from the Germans. This meant turning to the right and attacking almost 270 degrees from the direction in which they had been striving. Cherbourg was the port needed for the receiving of supplies vital to the newly landed army, and it had to be taken as soon as possible.

On June 14, two days after the division had received their new Commander, Landrum, the attack to the northwest — intended to seal the peninsula — jumped off. Little did Landrum know that his days were numbered. July 30 was to be his last with the 90th. It was at the time of the jump-off toward Cherbourg that the corps became aware that they were also facing the German 77th Division. As was expected, the going was believed to be rough.

It soon became apparent to the Germans that the prize the Allies sought was the port of Cherbourg. So much was the concern of Hitler that this prize not fall into the hands of the American 1st Army, that he ordered a staff conference to be held on June 17 to discuss, specifically, Cherbourg. Field Marshal Gerd von Rundstedt had installed a command post at Margival near Soissons in 1940, when the invasion of England was uppermost in German minds, and it was at this command post, now being used to defend the very lifeblood of Germany, that the conference was held. Von Rundstedt and Field Marshal Erwin Rommel (according to Lieutenant General Hans Spiedel) awaited the arrival of Hitler, who arrived with Colonel General Alfred Jodl. According to Edward Bauer, in *The History of World War II*, Rommel had gone by plane from Berchesgaden to Metz, then had traveled in an armored car.

> He looked pale and worn from lack of sleep. After a few cold words of greeting in a high and bitter voice, Hitler railed about the success of the Allied landings and blamed it on the local commanders. He ordered that Cherbourg be held at all costs.

Rommel was to serve as spokesman for both himself and for von Rundstedt, and he began by defending the leaders of the army from the vitriolic attacks just made by Hitler. He asserted that the first Allied thrust could have been thrown back into the sea only if the armored corps, which Hitler had held under his personal command, had been made available to von Rundstedt at the moment he had called so desperately for it. Hitler admitted that the Luftwaffe had not done what it should have to help resist the landings, but he promised that as soon as the new jet fighters came into production, they would completely control the battlefield. Again, acting as the spokesman of the two, Rommel said that it was believed that the Allies would swing north and west and take the Cotentin peninsula, then isolate Brittany, and then, freed from threats to their flanks, strike for Paris. He rejected the notion that there would be a second landing anywhere on the Channel and pleaded with Hitler to release the reserves that he held so that a war of maneuver could be conducted. To this plea Hitler gave his absolute refusal. As he saw it, the only way to defeat the Allies was to throw them back into the sea. There was to be no art of maneuver displayed, no quarter given.

Even while the meeting was taking place, the VII Corps' attack was clawing its way southward down the peninsula. The 82nd and the 9th were on either flank of the 90th, which was in the middle, lagging behind. In its sector, the 90th soon faced Hill #122 (Mont Castre), from which the Germans were directing artillery fire in the defense of the entire peninsula. It had to be taken by the Allies.

The peninsula of Cotentin is about 25 miles wide and 40 miles long, and at the northernmost extreme and in the center was the much coveted port of Cherbourg. In the center of the peninsula, and occupying virtually the entire southern portion of the land mass, was a sinister and forbidding area of waste land. As the land was close to sea level, much water stood at the surface of this area, known locally as Prairies Maracagéuses de Gorges. The peninsula was served by two main roads — one, paralleling the railroad, extended from Carentan through Valognes to Cherbourg, while the other extended from Granville on the Gulf of St. Malo through Coutances, Lessay, la Hayes-du-Puits, St. Sauveur-le-Vicomte, and to Valognes. Between the two roads there was no evidence of serious human habitation. There was a prominence just south of the village of la Hayes-du-Puits that was, according to the 90th Division history, "the commanding terrain feature of the entire peninsula and the enemy used it to good advantage." It afforded observation from which to direct artillery fire for a distance nearly from one side of the peninsula to the other. No wonder it was such a prize.

A principal German defense line, the Mahlberg Line, lay at the base of the peninsula, and it was against this that the VII Corps (with the 82nd and the 9th on either flank and the 90th in the middle) was about to attack. The goal for Collins's corps was to advance north and take the port. The corps advancing from the vicinity of the Normandy landing area first cut off and secured the peninsula and then swung to drive north. It had completed the drive to the coast when it encountered the Mahlberg Line.

The 4th Division (on the extreme left flank) pushed forward to the Gulf of St. Malo and was holding there, allowing the remaining three divisions of the corps to begin the completion of the work of reducing the peninsula.

It is interesting to speculate on what would be expected of the Commander of a line division under these, or any, battle conditions by the Army Commander. He would expect progress, steady and uniform, save where he believed resistance to be impenetrable. But the Army Commander would almost always judge performance of a division and of its Commander by the most swift and the most laggardly of those whom he could see. Again the unwritten military axiom applies: "Never fall too far to the rear nor advance too far in front." Clearly, the 90th was not staying in the shadows; it was doing its job without becoming a spectacle. Yet less than a month in combat, it was into its second Division Commander, and it was about to lose him because he stayed too far to the rear when he should have kept up.

The attack to secure the breakout from the coastal defenses of the German west wall began July 3, the day before Independence Day, with the 359th Regiment on the right and the 358th Regiment on the left; the 357th, in reserve, was to pass through the 358th to seize the famed Hill #122. The 1st Battalion of the 359th encountered a German force of like strength in plum orchards near the village of Pretot. The engagement soon evolved into close fighting among the trees, and when the time came to do so, the Germans retreated skillfully so that the Americans were to report that the opposition had been annihilated. (But because the ground that the attack had gained had been insignificant, the claim of annihilation was not taken seriously by the corps.) The 2nd Battalion was somewhat more successful, capturing the village of Ste. Suzanne, which it held at day's end.

The 1st Battalion of the 358th reached the crossroads north of St. Jore and while attempting to take the village was hit by six Tiger tanks, which began firing on the advancing troops from the concealment of the village. When the advance was halted, the tanks moved on the attackers, spoiling the assault. The attackers regrouped and tried again. The second time they were successful, and at nightfall they were in the village of St. Jore. A counterattack by the Germans had succeeded in taking the village of Les Sablons, which was attacked by the 3rd Battalion of the 358th at midday and retaken in order to close a gap between the 1st and 2nd Battalions. This day they had advanced about a thousand yards on the average.

July 4, Independence Day, saw the Germans still using Hill #122 to direct artillery on the striking American division. That day's attacks showed gains, though modest, and claimed the villages of Les Belle Croix and La Butte. The following day, the 357th (the division reserve) was committed for the purpose of breaking the Germans' hold on Hill #122, and by day's end one of its battalions had reached the foot of the hill and advanced to the highest ground on the north side of the forest. On the following day, the 357th advanced into Beau Caudray and held it with three companies of the 3rd Battalion. The 15th German Parachute Regiment attacked the village and quickly penetrated to positions behind the defending Americans. The attackers, sensing the opportunity of eating up a few Americans while defending the line, chose to do so. They pressed forward without respite, though they did allow a few riflemen and weapons soldiers to escape and report on what was about to happen.

The two remaining companies of the 3rd Battalion, isolated and unreachable, fought on until the night of July 7, when battalion radio became silent and the Mahlman Line remained intact. The 315th Engineers were committed into the line on the same day to make up for the loss of the 3rd Battalion of the 357th, for the Germans were counterattacking along the entire division front. The Germans were credited with launching five attacks that day, which, discounting small gains, were all repulsed. By July 8, the situation had become so frustrating that the 8th Infantry Division, which had been in corps reserve, was brought into the line west of the 90th, relieving pressure coming from this direction.

On July 8, the sixth day of attack and counterattack by the Germans, the 90th had begun to feel the effect of losing the infantry battalion in the face of serious German pressure. The historian of the division wrote that new units were formed of cooks, mechanics, and clerks, who took their places in the line and fought with concentrated fury. The next day was to see a resumption of attack and the first measure of success.

Rather late in the day, the 358th and 359th Infantry, having given up waiting for the 8th Infantry Division to arrive to assist in the offensive, attacked abreast against the Monte Castre. The 3rd Battalion of the 359th plunged into the woods in the Foret de Mont Castre, while its sister units (the 1st and 2nd Battalions) were simply unable to advance on the enemy in their front.

For the 3rd Battalion, this day was to be especially trying. This was the seventh time that Americans had tried to dislodge the German defenders from the woods of Monte Castre. The forward units of the battalion advanced into the woods with but token resistance from the defenders. The most difficult obstacles to their advance were the dense woods and the rocky terrain. Visibility was poor to nil, and most of the soldiers became hopelessly disoriented. At times, it was impossible to ascertain where the firing was coming from or who was doing it. It was not a favorable place in which to attack or to defend.

When the first forest objective seemed to have been reached, the battalion pressed forward. Suddenly, all hell broke loose. Machine guns, which had remained silent until the attackers were almost upon them, opened up and from commanding positions raked the woods. Grenades came from individuals concealed in earthen holes. Rifle fire from the defenders was more accurate than from the attackers, and hence casualties were disproportionate. The only thing left for the attackers to do was to charge, though just what to charge was not certain. But charge they did, and again, and again. All day long the men of the 3rd Battalion fought the German defenders in close quarters in that tiny piece of wooded terrain. When darkness finally fell, the stretcher bearers came up and retrieved the wounded. The casualties of the 3rd Battalion were 52 percent taken that bloody day. No longer would the unit fight as three line companies and a heavy weapons and a Headquarters company; now they would all line up together, for their numbers had become so few.

On the seventh day of continuous attack, the 358th and 357th again met with fierce opposition. But finally, the German resistance began to soften, and it seemed, even to the weary attackers, that victory was possible — or rather gaining the assigned objectives was possible. On this day, July 9, the Mahlman Line was broken, and the 90th advanced beyond its sanctuary.

With the German 15th Parachute Regiment dislodged, the assault was temporarily over and the 90th took a breather. But a new offensive by the

Americans was forthcoming. The general objective was to drive the German defenders from the Cherbourg peninsula and onto the plains of France. The order of battle placed the U.S. VII Corps on the left and the VIII Corps on the right. The 90th Division was to drive south of Periers along the road. In the way of this advance was a remnant German position astride the road known to the attackers as "the island." This entrenched position — looking like a football lost of air — was so named because it was surrounded by terrain features that, like water around an island, made the position inaccessible. On the north it was bounded by the river Seves, while on the other sides it was bounded by swamp. The only reasonable approach was across the river, and the only avenue to the river was across open ground, under German surveillance.

Following an intense barrage of seemingly well-placed artillery, the 1st and 2nd Battalions of the 358th made the assault on the "island." As there was little action on the Normandy front this day (July 9), the German defenders were able to mass artillery for the defense of the "island." Across open fields the 90th attackers converged. As they came in range, automatic weapons fire railed upon them from the southern bank of the Seves. In the morning of the attack, one company of the 1st Battalion gained and held access to the far side of the Seves; however, under heavy fire they withdrew before noon.

In the afternoon, the 1st Battalion again forced a crossing and for a time made some progress into the "island." But mortar and automatic weapons fire was so intense that the engineers could not bridge the river and no armor was available to support the embattled attackers. After dark, a line company of the 2nd Battalion was able to come across and lend its support to the attack on the Germans. The attackers were able to resist a staunch German counterattack, which was launched late in the evening.

When morning came, the perverse "god of the battlefield" decided to see what the attackers would do in the face of some real odds. Rain began to fall and after a bit the Seves River left its banks and spread, so that supplying the attackers was not possible and bridging the river was simply out of the question. The beachhead was at an end. Those who could swim did so and, if they were not drowned in the swift current, made it safely back to American lines. Those who could not swim simply stayed and eventually became German prisoners. In a few short days, the division had lost the equivalent of two of its nine battalions, and it was short of its second objective.

There was then a time for pause and reflection. The 90th licked its wounds. It had from July 15 until July 26 to do so. On the 26th, and now assigned to the VIII Corps, which also included the 79th, 8th, and 83rd Divisions, the 90th attacked south toward Coutances. The VII Corps on the left quickly took St. Lo. When the city fell, the situation in front of Coutances became obvious to the German defenders. If they remained and defended the line that they occupied, the swiftly moving VII Corps stood a very good chance of flanking them and pinning them against the sea at the Gulf of St. Malo. Prudent as they were, the Germans withdrew, and by the evening that St. Lo fell, July 16, Periers also fell, having been abandoned by the defenders.

All this time, General Omar Bradley had been watching the 90th to see how Landrum was doing, waiting, not any too patiently, for him to stumble. In summation, it had finally happened. The 90th had been "lackluster" slow and had been the tail of the VIII Corps. In addition to all that, the division had lost nearly a quarter of its strength in rifle troops during a scant two months of fighting, more than the average casualties sustained by Normandy divisions. Bradley wrote in *A General's Story*,

> Landrum had not yet got the ill-trained 90th Division in fighting trim. He had cleaned house but not enough. I was compelled to relieve him.

And then in an almost unbelievable passage, no doubt written to salve his conscience for having sacked Theodore Roosevelt, of the 1st Infantry Division, in Sicily. Bradley wrote that he felt that, Roosevelt's

> magnificent performance on Utah Beach had earned him command of a division and decided to give him the 90th. As I was in the process of clearing this appointment with Ike, I learned to my shock and sorrow that Teddy Roosevelt had died in his sleep of a heart attack.

The serious reader of military history will soon learn that the selection of a replacement Commander hardly follows "let the most able step forward" or "let the office seek the man." Usually, long before the sacking, the replacement has been chosen and is being groomed for the takeover once it can be orchestrated properly. There is really no likelihood that

Bradley would have given the 90th Division to Teddy Roosevelt, had he lived. Roosevelt was too much an individual for the likings of Bradley, who, like all great captains, sought all glory to himself.

So Bradley decided to play the politic and selected General Raymond McLain, the artillery general of the 45th. This was a shrewd move, for it placated those in Congress who chafed at the rigid control held by graduates of the U.S. Military Academy. If McLain, vice president of a prestigious Oklahoma City bank, were even remotely successful with his newly acquired division, the next step would be to push him up to the command of a corps, where he could surely do no one harm.

This selection reflects contorted logic. General Jay McKelvie could not handle the 90th Division because "he was an artillery specialist," yet General Raymond McLain was selected "because of the outstanding job he had done as commander of the artillery of the 45th Division."

History tells little of the fate of Gene Landrum. He, who had been a good Chief of Staff to the wonderboy J. Lawton Collins, had failed a menial task. He had lost 20 percent of his dogfaced infantrymen and had little to show for it. Better had he stayed in his safe place in Corps Headquarters — but perhaps he had no choice.

Chapter 10

Jones and the Short Life of the Golden Lion

*A*LAN W. JONES *was born in 1894 in Golden, Colorado, and commissioned second lieutenant, U.S. Infantry, in June 1917. He was immediately promoted to first lieutenant. Too late to serve overseas in World War I, during hostilities he saw duty in Kansas and Florida. In 1922, he was transferred to the Philippines to serve in the 45th Infantry. Returning to the United States the following year, he attended the Infantry School at Fort Ben-*

ning, Georgia, first as a student in the basic course, then as an instructor and student in the advanced course. He went immediately to the Artillery School in 1930 and was graduated the following year, when he was posted with the 12th Infantry in Maryland. In 1935, he entered the Command and General Staff School at Fort Leavenworth, Kansas, and on graduation in 1936, he joined the 7th Infantry in Washington State. In 1937, he entered the Army War College at Carlisle Barracks, Pennsylvania, and graduated the following year, when he was assigned to the 19th Infantry in Hawaii.

When Jones returned to the mainland in 1941, he was assigned to G-3 (Operations and Training) of the General Staff in Washington. He then went to the Army Ground Forces Command and from there to the 90th Infantry Division, then in its training cycle. He was promoted to brigadier general and became Assistant Division Commander. When the 106th Infantry Division was activated in South Carolina, Alan Jones received his second star and became the Commander, taking the division to Europe.

A heart attack on the day he was relieved of command resulted in his evacuation, eventually to Walter Reed Army Hospital in Washington, D.C. There he remained until he was able to be retired at his permanent rank of lieutenant colonel.

The 106th Infantry Division, which wore the shoulder patch of a Golden Lion, was activated on March 15, 1943, and deactivated in 1946. It served less than a month in the line against the Germans. It was attacked, overrun, and partially decimated, and it finally lost, by capture, more than half the remaining division strength. The Division Commander, Major General Alan W. Jones, was relieved of command by his Corps Commander, Major General Matthew B. Ridgway, and within the night had suffered a heart attack that was to end, mercifully, his Army career.

In the halcyon days of the Golden Lion (1944), photographs were taken and assembled of every soldier and officer of the division for a keepsake book. In the book there appears a picture of Jones and Lieutenant General Lloyd Fredendall. It is interesting to note that just a few months before the picture was taken, Fredendall himself had been relieved of command for his accomplishments (or lack thereof) at Kasserine in North Africa;

Major General Alan W. Jones, who was relieved of command of the ill-fated 106th (Golden Lion) Division after two-thirds of his command was captured in the fierce fighting of the Battle of the Bulge. (U.S. Army Signal Corps)

Ironically, for him there was a promotion on the other side of the ocean, when he returned to America, relieved of command, he was promptly promoted to lieutenant general. If permitted and so inclined, the Army looks after its own.

The infantry, artillery, medics, and engineers of the Golden Lion were all brought into the division in the time-honored way. First, a cadre of non-commissioned officers was selected from a trained and seasoned unit. In the case of the 106th, the cadre was from the 80th Infantry Division, which was just completing final training and about to be sent to Europe. Contrasting with practice at the time (when units were activated and assigned to a division and bore some numerical semblance to the parent division), several existing units were amalgamated into the Golden Lion: the 106th Quartermaster Company, the 860th Ordnance Company, and the 106th Division Artillery Band and 423rd Infantry Band (both formerly National Guard unit bands; their unit designations were simply changed). Alan W. Jones, who was at the time the Assistant Division Commander of the 90th (Texas-Oklahoma) Division, was promoted to major general and became the Commander of the 106th. The Assistant Division Commander, Brigadier General Herbert T. Perrin, had served in the 1st Infantry Division (Big Red One) in World War I. The Chief of Staff was Colonel William C. Baker.

Basic and unit training for the division took place at Fort Jackson, South Carolina. Afterward, the division was to enjoy the opportunity to participate in maneuvers, with the 2nd Army in Tennessee. At any other time, it would seem odd that participation in maneuvers would be a privilege, but at the time, troop needs in Europe were so great and the shortage so acute that most divisions were sent directly to the front without this benefit of the combined maneuver. In addition, most infantry divisions that were training and preparing for combat eventually were stripped of soldiers, who were to be replacements for overseas losses. The divisions would have to begin unit training anew, and thus they never reached the state of readiness that would have qualified them to participate in maneuvers.

For the 106th Infantry Division, the "replacement axe" fell after (rather than before) they had completed maneuvers, while they were at Camp Atterbury, Indiana, awaiting their call to combat. By June 1944, more than 60 percent of the division's enlisted strength had been requisitioned as replacements. These troops were replaced by new drafts and by college students from the Army Student Training Program (ASTP). (Before it was abolished in 1944, the ASTP was considered the haven for college men who preferred to bend an elbow and visit the sorority houses than to peel potatoes and force march in the rain.) It was then up to the remaining officers and noncoms of the division to take what had been left and what was

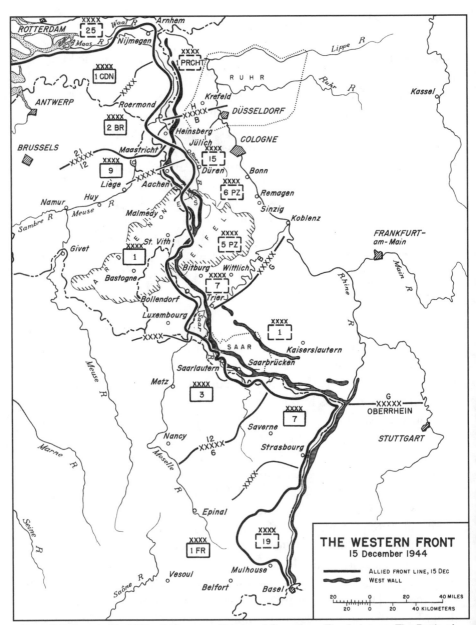

From *U.S. Army in World War II: European Theater of Operations, The Ardennes: The Battle of the Bulge*, by Hugh M. Cole (Washington, D.C.: U.S. Army, Office of the Chief of Military History, 1965), 52.

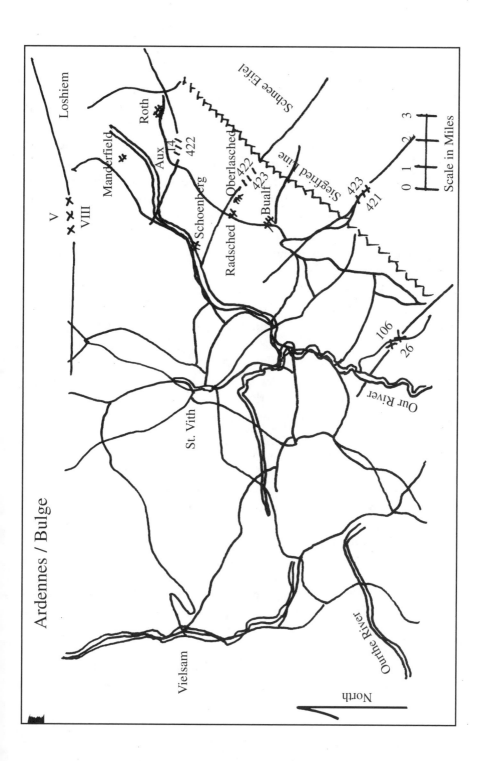

Ardennes / Bulge

given and make a fighting division before October 1944, when the division began to move to England.

The 106th remained for a month in England until December 1, 1944, when it crossed the Channel and immediately boarded open truck-trailers to be driven to the front, a sector occupied by the VIII Corps.

On December 7, the 106th Infantry Division took over lock, stock, and barrel from the 2nd (Indian Head) Division. The 106th got guns and machine artillery from the 2nd and gave the 2nd theirs; they then occupied the same huts, foxholes, bunkers, houses, and buildings as had the men of the 2nd. The Indian Heads called that segment of the line a "rest camp," and right they should, for there, on a ridge known as Schnee Eifel, no real fighting had occurred since the area had been taken back in September by the 4th Infantry Division.

As the 106th came into the line, the 28th Division (of the VIII Corps) was on the right flank of the 424th Infantry Regiment (the rightmost regiment of the 106th), which occupied seven miles of front. On the left, the 423rd occupied nearly the same, and on its left, the 422nd occupied a somewhat reduced front of about five miles. The division front was rounded out with the 14th Cavalry Group (an attached unit from the VIII Corps) occupying a front of nearly five miles. All told, the division occupied a front of 24 miles (at a time when most textbooks would advise that an infantry division occupy a front of about 15 miles).

Major General Jones had been told, and ordered in writing, to assume a role of "aggressive defense" with readiness to advance on Cologne on orders of the 1st Army. Those first few days of the 106th at the frontline position were no doubt filled with apprehension, as the men wondered what would happen. As the days wore on, they probably began to get accustomed to being there and to feel some comfort, even a little security. Of course, in such circumstances there is typically the Commanding General who is incessantly ordering combat patrols to go out and "capture some prisoners" and engineer patrols to go out and "test the enemy fortifications and his mine fields." It was always thought by the troops that if one was not killed with such "Tom Foolery," one would probably provoke the enemy who would retaliate and then there would be all hell to pay.

Major General Jones, like all his counterparts in all those 100-odd divisions that made up the U.S. Army, was also probably given to patrols and active defense, for he had no doubt heard that this was the way to get his division's "feet wet." It is hardly likely that his activity annoyed the Ger-

106th Division
infantryman on patrol
in the Battle of the
Bulge. (U.S. Army
Signal Corps)

mans though, for they had other things on their minds. If, by chance, his patrols had reported on all that they had seen (columns of trucks and supplies, as well as armor moving up) and his S-2s and his G-2 had believed what they were being told — and had these Intelligence officers been convincing and had they convinced anyone, up to division, that a big thing was about to come off — then, and only perhaps then, two reserve divisions would have been found to support the corps, and the Battle of the Bulge might have been blunted ere it claimed the life of the Golden Lion Division.

106th Division Headquarters was in St. Vith. Before sunup, on December 16, artillery shells began to fall on it, 12 miles from the front and 20 miles from the closest place the Germans would put heavy artillery. At precisely the same time, artillery began to fall on every unit, strategic location, crossroad, bridge, and target of believed value within the division area. At 6:15 a.m., when the barrage ceased, German infantry (clad in white to blend with the snow) began to advance along the entire front.

In the autumn of 1944, the Germans had been convinced that unless something bold and upsetting were done, the Allies would continue to advance into Germany and the Russians would continue their relentless drive from the east, for the Russians were, even at that time, threatening East Prussia, Poland, and Germany. The Balkans lay in shambles, and virtually all that had been gained had been lost. A bold stroke — one that would upset the Allied timetable — had to be made; and what could be more stunning than for the Allies to lose Antwerp, their premier port on the North Sea, where entered all that fed the hungry machine that was their land army? The German high command — Colonel General Alfred Jodl and Field Marshal Wilhelm Keitel — believed that Germany could muster the resources to launch and succeed in this Antwerp effort.

Germany realized with pain that she was incapable of mounting any effort that would in any way affect the Russians. And so it came to be that the decision was made and plans laid to attack again at the same location, on the same ground, with the same Commander (Field Marshal Gerd von Rundstedt), and with the same goal (drive to the coast and eliminate Belgium) as had been done when the blitzkrieg carried France away in 1940. This lofty effort had the code name Herbstenebel (Autumn Fog).

The position in the line of the 106th Infantry Division was on what was to become the southern shoulder of the German attack. The German Order of Battle for those units that engaged the 106th U.S. Infantry Division was the 1st Panzer Army, commanded by Colonel General Hasso von Manteuffel; the LXVI Corps, formed in 1942 as a reserve corps and destined to be one of the most successful units to be engaged in the Bulge; the 18th Volksgrenadier Division, comprised of the 293rd, 294th, and 295th Grenadier Regiments, 1818th Artillery Regiment, 18th Fusilier Battalion, 1818th Engineer Battalion, 1818th Anti-Tank Battalion, 1818th Signal Battalion, and the remnants of the 18th Luftwaffe Field Division; the 62nd Volksgrenadier Division, consisting of the 164th, 183rd, and 190th Infantry Regiments, 162nd Artillery Regiment, and 162nd Battalion of Reconnaissance, Engineers, Anti-Tank, and Signals; and the 116th Panzer Division, comprised of the 116th Panzer Battalion, 60th and 156th Panzer Grenadier Regiments, 146th Motorized Artillery Regiment, 59th Motorcycle Battalion, 116th Panzer Reconnaissance Battalion, 146th Anti-Tank Battalion, 116th Engineer Battalion, and 228th Motorized Signal Battal-

Members of the 106th Division being marched into a POW camp. (Captured Wehrmacht photograph)

American equipment abandoned and burning during the retreat of the Battle of the Bulge. (Captured Wehrmacht photograph)

ion. The 116th Panzer Division had also merged with the 179th Reserve Panzer. Though it had fewer than 50 tanks total, the division was the spearhead in the attack.

Though there was forward movement by the Germans all along the front, it would seem that the greater pressure at that time was probably at the northern part of the 106th Division area, with a concentration of intensity near the village of Losheim. All day long the attack came, but nowhere was the situation in danger. Major General Jones was said to have commented that the 106th Infantry Division had "been tried" that day and would be even more so the next. When darkness came, the Allied soldiers expected to stop fighting, build a fire, cook a bit of food, post some outposts, sing a few songs, and go to sleep. But the Germans continued to attack — all night.

Generally, the line the Golden Lion had inherited from the Indian Head occupied high, commanding terrain, in the center of the division front, while to the north and to the south the land was more gentle and inviting, particularly to an attacker. Roads ran parallel to and, in some instances, along the front. Roads normal to this axis, though of the same caliber, were equally spaced across the division front — about five of them. The terrain was everywhere heavily wooded, impeding the tanks' advance from any direction. Such vehicles would, of necessity, be confined to the roads. But as these forests precluded the passage of armor, so too they gave the cover and, sometimes, the protection needed for infantry concealment and advancement. The gentle terrain to the north and south invited tanks and armored vehicular thrusts. Germany, having used these woods to their advantage in an attack in World War I, could be expected to try to repeat the success.

Alan Jones had chosen to place his three infantry regiments (the 422nd, 423rd, and 424th) and his attached cavalry group (the 14th) side-by-side along the line. He had retained but one infantry battalion as a division reserve. The frontline Regimental Commanders had more wisely chosen to place one of their battalions in reserve.

Throughout the second day of the attack, the Germans continued to exert pressure all along the front. Toward the end of the day there was a thrust at the north, at the point of Losheim. It should have been obvious to Major General Jones that it was the German's intention to penetrate far enough to swing left and cut off the bulk of the 106th Division. Of course, this was not the primary purpose of the attack; it was to push forward and secure the port of Antwerp and deny the Allies that major source of supply for the northern part of their front.

The weather at the time was terrible — snow and heavy gray skies with low clouds. Then, there was the inability of the Allies to put planes in the sky. No sorties flew, and the Germans continued to advance and bring up reinforcements, unseen. As would be expected, the battlefield was in a state of confusion. The Germans somehow had been able to tap into Allied telephone lines and probably had been doing so for some time. The Indian Head Division, which had taken over for a division already in the line, had not bothered to check the security of communications, and the 106th, arrived only lately, had also not done so. They simply had not had the time. This breach of security is believed to have allowed Germany to listen to Allied talk on telephone lines, and they exploited their newly obtained knowledge.

German penetration continued during the second night and the third day in the vicinity of Losheim. As the hours wore on, it became apparent that the Germans were not being contained. Meanwhile, constant pressure of the lines along the ridge was making headway. Little incursions here and there were cutting units from communication. At this time, the Division Headquarters was not exercising control over the units under its command. Most of the artillery was operating separately. Infantry frequently called on the artillery for firing missions, particularly point-blank fire on German tanks.

While the 1st, 2nd, and 3rd Battalions of the 422nd Infantry occupied side-by-side positions along the Schnee Eifel (which ran northeast/southwest), the 14th Cavalry Group to the north occupied the less favorable terrain, which later became known as the Losheim Gap. The major thrust advanced there, which ultimately sealed the fate of the surrounded regiments that surrendered.

The Our River ran through this sector. It was surrounded by a broad, flat valley, in the center of which was the village of Manderfeld. If the village fell, the entire rear of the 422nd Infantry would be open; if exploited by a determined attacker, so would that of the 423rd Infantry, which occupied ridge positions on the right flank. Unbelievably, this seven-mile front was occupied only by a cavalry group, with some corps artillery support, and the actual occupation of the front line consisted of only a squadron of cavalry while the other squadron remained in support to the rear. In contrast, the infantry had mainly committed all of its forces to frontline positions.

In defense of the cavalry, it must be said that it was responding to a role for which it was unsuited. Seven miles of valley and ridge front occupied by 1,000 soldiers in lightly armored vehicles is quite different from the seven miles of mountainous crest occupied by 3,000 well-entrenched infantry men. The 14th Cavalry Group did have supporting it a portion of the 820th Tank Destroyers.

Surprisingly, Alan Jones was not worried as to the condition of his division. During the third day of the attack, and with penetrations into the Vorsheim (the gently rolling land behind the ridge, which was the center position of the division), he called on the VIII Corps for help. When he was assured that he would receive an uncommitted cavalry group and that an infantry division was on its way to assist him, he became calm and complacent, as if all was well.

The first progress that the German attack made was to penetrate the 14th Cavalry and swing south on the road that led to Aux. By midday of December 18, the town was in German hands. Hearing nothing from units that had previously been reporting, Colonel Charles Descheneaux, Commander of the 422nd Infantry Regiment, sent foot patrols to make contact with whoever held the village; they discovered that it was occupied by the Germans. The 422nd responded by attacking toward Aux with an infantry company and with the cannon company. Although they could not regain the lost village, they at least stopped the German advance to the south toward Radscheid. The division reserve, the 2nd Battalion of the 423rd Infantry, commanded by Lieutenant Colonel Joseph Puett, was being held in bivouac at Born. It was ordered to take the allotted trucks and move south to St. Vith and then east to secure the village of Schoenburg. Puett secured the village and while doing so met nearby cavalry and artillery units of the division and attached units retreating as he was occupying. Soon he came under heavy German artillery fire. As the cavalry was withdrawing, Puett warned the Commander that if Schoenburg fell, the 422nd and 423rd would be cut off.

Puett communicated his position and predicament in Schoenburg. But by the time the news of Puett's heavy engagement was sinking in at the Division Headquarters, the seriousness of this location paled in comparison with the plight of the 422nd Infantry right flank, which was being threatened by German penetration. Puett's 2nd Battalion was instructed to advance to the southeast and protect the right of the 422nd and to move to what division called the "high ground south of Aux." In complying with this order, Puett moved south until the road running northeast along the Schnee Eifel was encountered. There he turned north and secured a position on the rear slope of the ridge occupied by the 1st and 3rd Battalions of his regiment.

Meanwhile, Jones had been promised by the VIII Corps that he would be reinforced by a combat command of the 7th Armored Division when it arrived. He continued to await that arrival. The first soldiers that he saw from the 7th were not what he anticipated; they were merely the advance party of a unit not expected to reach the 106th Division area for another 24 hours. When the combat command of the 7th did arrive, it was too late to save the 106th. Two of its infantry regiments were by then cut off and could not have been extricated with less force than an armored corps.

The name "Skyline Drive" was given to the road that connected the installations of the Siegfried Line (the fortified German line stretching from Belgium to the Swiss border) atop the ridge/mountain range that extended to the northeast and southwest and was the strong position occupied by the frontline units of the 422nd and 423rd Infantries. Shortly after its arrival, the 2nd Battalion, 423rd Infantry, was ordered to take up position in the line, adjacent to the 1st. All the next day, units of the 423rd were under heavy German attack, as was the 422nd on its left and the 424th on its right. Colonel Cavender, 423rd Regimental Commander, had learned that enemy troops had secured Schoenburg, and he was told to turn his regiment around and attack to relieve this village. To do this, the rearward-moving battalions passed directly on the flank of the embattled Puett. As this attack to Schoenburg was underway, Major General Jones, of 106th Division Staff, ordered Cavender to attack Schoenburg, do maximum damage to the enemy there, and then proceed to attack toward St. Vith. It was said to be of "grave importance to the nation" to secure St. Vith.

This order was indeed a little silly. The 423rd was three miles from Schoenburg, its initial objective, and another seven miles from St. Vith. The 423rd could hardly keep the Germans from overrunning its present position. Cavender did what he thought best and at the same time attempted to carry out orders. He began attacking and moving troops so that he would concentrate the regiment at Radscheid, having withdrawn from a similarly precarious position near Oberlascheid. The 422nd was falling back from Skyline Drive to positions around Schlausenbach. These two moves were virtually the last of these two doomed regiments; thereafter, they would shift a bit — the 423rd would even attempt an attack — but they would remain where they were.

Cavender decided to disengage the 2nd and 3rd Battalions from their confrontations with the Germans, yet the 2nd was under attack. But, instead of getting the 3rd to help the 2nd as it passed by, the 3rd was ordered to move on to Schoenburg, the regimental first objective. The 2nd Battalion remained occupied at Radscheid while the 1st and 3rd advanced a bit farther forward. Toward nightfall on the 18th, the units of the 423rd began to be concentrated at a point in the valley between Schoenburg and Oberlascheid. Meanwhile, the 422nd, ordered to attack and take Schoenburg, began moving from the position it had occupied when it withdrew from the front, a position three miles southeast of the village. The remnants of the two regiments were about to converge at their regimental boundary on the road north of Radscheid. In these maneuvers, the 2nd Battalion of the 423rd found itself among the 422nd, and Puett chose to cast his lot with them. They were entering a perimeter defense. Artillery was pounding the perimeter, and Puett decided to set off on a foot reconnaissance to try to find a way out of the mess.

The Germans had cut off all American troops east of the Our River. All surrounded troops were in isolated and separated perimeter defense positions. In accordance with time-honored practice, the Germans began to shell the isolated pockets to encourage the defenders to give up. Mixing air bursts with ground bursts, German artillerymen were beginning to fray the nerves of the Allied infantrymen huddled in foxholes. The trees of the forest had been shredded, and the men seemed to be sentenced to die where they were, for they could neither advance nor withdraw.

Colonel Descheneaux, the 422nd Commander, had allowed his medics to choose a location for the battalion aid station that was within both sight and hearing of his battalion command post. He could see the mounting casualties and hear their cries. He knew that he had no means of getting relief for them, because there was no means of evacuation. He had been promised relief in the form of the 7th Armored Division, but it had not arrived; he came to believe that it would not arrive. He had also been promised resupply from an air drop, but neither had this come. Nor could he rouse Division Headquarters due to constant German jamming of the radio channels. The sounds of the wounded were certainly a factor that influenced his thinking at this most critical time in his military career. What would have been his choice had he only seen his dead, rather than heard the cries of the wounded?

Having decided to surrender, Descheneaux sent Major Cody Garlow of Puett's 2nd Battalion — without Puett's knowledge — to seek out the Germans. He would go under a white flag of truce to find a German commander to whom they could surrender. When an English-speaking German officer had been found by Garlow, the little party of victor and vanquished returned to effect the surrender.

Independently, 200 yards away, Cavender of the 423rd Infantry had also reached the end of his rope. Puett had disappeared into the mist, and Lieutenant Colonel Klinck's 3rd had over 50 percent casualties. The 1st had been reduced to remnants that were by then fighting with other units to which they had attached themselves.

With Descheneaux's and Cavender's surrender that afternoon of December 19, 7,000 men of the Golden Lion and attached units became prisoners of Germany. Because the infantry comprises the heart of a division, the loss of two of the three regiments of the 106th meant that the division had lost two-thirds of its capability.

The story is told — though it may simply be a bit of legend — that as these troops were being marched away to the railhead that would take them to the German prisoner-of-war camp, many of them began removing from the shoulder of their jackets the Golden Lion.

With the surrender of the surrounded 422nd and 423rd Infantry Regiments in perimeter defense a scant mile in diameter, it became imperative that relief — in the form of the armored division that was supposed to rescue the remainder — come before their resources were expended and their Commanders saw the situation as hopeless. The constant jamming by the Germans continued to make communication with Division Headquarters nearly impossible.

Meanwhile, sensing the turmoil that existed on his front and realizing the likelihood that St. Vith itself would be engulfed, Major General Alan Jones chose wisely to move his command post to the rear — Vielsalm. The equally hard-pressed, but yet functioning, 424th Infantry was holding to its positions, giving ground where needed but remaining intact. It had on its flank the reliable 28th Keystone Division. Of course, the main German thrust, while willing to exploit any weakness found at this location, was not really interested in advancing in this direction. Their desire was penetration first, deep penetration, and then exploitation in order to achieve their goal of Antwerp.

The massive German penetration had not gone unnoticed by the Allied command, which was trying desperately to stem the tide of advance. Unused and resting troops were found and started on their way to St. Vith. They began to arrive at about the time the 422nd and 423rd Regiments were being surrounded and put to their final test. The situation had become so desperate so quickly that Army Commanders — and even General Eisenhower, the theater Commander — came to believe that some changes in command were needed. General Matthew Ridgway and the XVIII Airborne Corps surveyed the situation and realized that it was unlikely that they could, with the resources at hand, extricate the surrounded regiments of the 106th. Furthermore, there was the problem of stemming the main German thrust before it could penetrate deeper. Nevertheless, if resources allowed, Ridgway would try to get the surrounded regiments out. It was for this reason, at least partially, that he summoned Alan Jones to his Headquarters on the night of December 22.

British Field Marshal Sir Bernard Montgomery, Commander of the 21st Army Group, had sent observers to the area of Vielsalm to ascertain the extent of the German incursion and to help in selecting a meaningful defense line that could be held. Major General Robert W. Hasbrouck, commanding the newly arrived 7th Armored Division and attempting to hold the area in which the 106th was surrendering, was of the mind that the line should be retired before his division was surrounded also and ceased to exist. Ridgway believed that the line on which he stood could be held, and he was pressing to do so. As he toured the area and spoke with Colonel Reid, commanding the yet-viable 424th Infantry, Brigadier General Bruce Clark, the Armor Commander, and General William M. Hoge of Combat Command B of the 9th Armored Division, Ridgway was formulating the scene that would take place later at Hasbrouck's headquarters in Vielsalm.

When Ridgway summoned Major General Jones to Hasbrouck's command post, he queried him about his perception of the situation. Jones seemed unduly optimistic. He had lost two-thirds of his division and had his remaining infantry regiment, the 424th, fighting a coordinated defense with the attached 116th Infantry of the 28th Division. Yet Jones was talking of grand plans to extricate units that were either nonexistent or about to surrender. After the interview, Ridgway summoned Hasbrouck and in his presence relieved Jones of his command, assigning Hasbrouck the command of the remaining troops of the 106th, as well as his own, and of the other unattached troops in the area.

Jones seemingly took the relief in stride and began arranging to turn over the command. Shortly afterward, he retired to bed while others pondered on the sorry condition of the battlefield. In the night, he awakened with chest pains; his aide called for a medic. The pain was diagnosed as a severe coronary. An ambulance was summoned, which took him to the rear, away from the division that he — and Commanders above him and staff Intelligence officers — had allowed to be decimated.

Probably, there are few military situations warranting critique that absolve the participants of blame for failure, but the Golden Lion in the Bulge may be one of them. Few, and perhaps none, of the very grand divisions of the European theater would have been expected to do much differently than did the 106th.

Had Major General Jones received authorization to withdraw if he was forced to do so in order to forestall capture? None of those in the chain of command has ever faulted him for not retreating when he had the opportunity. We must believe that none, from Eisenhower down, had thought retreat was an option. Jones had been told to hold.

It is possible to draw an analogy between this case and that of Major General Charles Gordon, British defender of the doomed garrison in Khartoum. He kept his troops with high hope because until the very end he could assure them that help was on the way. It did not save the garrison, which was finally overwhelmed. But it did give them courage and comfort to believe that they had not been forgotten.

But the analogy falters when it comes to Bataan and, certainly, Corregidor. Until it was too late for the soldiers to do anything about their situation, they thought that MacArthur was in it with them. When he left, ostensibly under orders, it was a day of infamy for the Commander who had intimated that he would remain with his troops.

But as for the 106th Infantry Division, anyone who has ever been in the infantry in combat can certainly say of the 106th at St. Vith and the Schnee Eifel, "There but for the grace of God go I."

Conclusion

*T*HIS BOOK SPEAKS of little con-
flicts, not of grand strategy. Interestingly, it is those little, insignificant incursions that draw the interest and the insistence of leaders — comfortable elsewhere — who demand that more be
given. If these battles which I have written
about had never occurred, the course of des-
tiny would not have changed. These battles
were, in the main, isolated battle scenes,

so detached from the real world of the moment that they stand, glaringly.

The men who are written about were guided by their chosen profession (men of arms) to offer themselves. They were not unlike their peers. They were dedicated, loyal, brave, and well-trained in their craft. They had performed well in the preparatory tasks that qualified them for this final testing.

Chance has played a great part in their undoing, yet chance has favored others. So chance, in itself, must be discounted. These men have lacked boldness and replaced it with correctness and caution. They simply did not achieve what was expected of them. As levels of expectation ever change, so must the leader ever change the expectation of himself. He must outthink his superior and, if he dare to succeed, dare to fail. None of the leaders that I have written about have done this.

History will give them but a footnote — "He was relieved." But as to notoriety, they have probably achieved more in the historical context than have their peers who succeeded. There were nearly 150 Division and Corps Commanders of the World War II American Army. Most of them performed quite well and, in doing so, won the war. Yet, for all their good work, only a handful are known, even to the student of military history. But the few who failed are remembered.

There is irony in this bitter truth. For the inspiring soldier of tomorrow there is an admonition: "Never select the Little Big Horn. If you are chosen to rest there, decline. For in so doing you will live to fight another day."

There are two incidents in which Army general officers have been relieved by those of other services. General Brown was relieved at Attu by the U.S. Navy because the prolonged conflict on land endangered their battleship, which they did not want to lose in such an insignificant engagement. Of course, it was not germane, at least in the mind of the Navy, that their battleship had been of no appreciable benefit to the campaign, and, in one incidence, had been requested to remain silent by the Ground Commander. The Navy could have sent the battleship away and let Brown take whatever time was necessary to silence the enemy. Theirs was a sorry action.

Then there is the matter of Ralph Smith of the Army and Holland Smith of the Marines. Smith of the Marines was lying in wait for Smith of the Army, remembering him from the "last movie in which he played" and already determined that he would relieve him. In this case, there was absolutely nothing that Ralph Smith could have done differently that would have saved him.

Much the same can be said of Major General Terry de la Mesa Allen of the Big Red One and General Omar Bradley. After the Tunisian riot by the 1st, Bradley had decided to let Allen go; he only waited to get the last bit of good out of him before letting him go. But if there was one who reaped where he did not sow, it was Bradley. He fished for praise for his work yet condemned others who fished for praise for their work (*i.e.*, Patton and Eisenhower). In his writings, after the fact, and when he could get nothing else from Eisenhower, he writes snide words of the man who made him what he was. Bradley, who was carefully cautious in his own professional and personal actions, found caution as one of the several reasons that he used to relieve the 20-odd general officers whom he sacked. Not to be confined to those whom he could sack (his subordinates), he also implied in his writings that many of those who were equal to or greater than he should go (*i.e.*, Jake Devers, Patton, Alexander, Eisenhower, Tedder, Coningham, Montgomery, to name a few).

Ego plays heavily in the makeup of general officers, and no less in the makeup of those who sack. Allen probably would have never gotten on Bradley's list had his Division not gotten Bradley chewed out for the Tunisian rioting. Ego plays heavily in the perception that general officers have of the supposed adulation in which they are held by their men. Having read the thoughts of corps, Army, and Army Group Commanders concerning the love and loyalty which their soldiers have for them, I have put this proposition to philosophic scrutiny. My findings? From the perspective of a combat engineer platoon in combat, I have attempted to assay the pride/comradeship/allegiance that the soldier feels for his ascending levels of command, from the pinnacle of his squad to the pinnacle of his country. The table below lists what I believe to be true.

Pride/Comradeship/Allegiance of a Soldier to Ascending Levels of Command (%)

Squad	100	Division	90
Platoon	90	Corps	0
Company	80	Army	60
Battalion	70	Army Group	0
Regiment	50	His Country	100

If the above be true, then it could be explain why a Commander cannot abide a subordinate Commander who is too greatly loved by his men.

Another perception is derived from the study of sacking of general officers. Those Commanders who have not smelled cordite (*i.e.*, been battlefield Commanders) are more likely to be a sacker than those who have been in battle, at the level of the one they might sack. Omar Bradley, who had never commanded a division in combat, never commanded any real fighting force in combat, was the worst sacker of World War II.

Bibliography

The Aleutian Campaign. Navy Historical Center, Department of the Navy, 1993.

Allen, William Lusk, *Anzio: Edge of Disaster*. Elsevier-Dutton, 1978.

Battle of the Bulge. Bison Books, 1983.

Bauer, Edward, *The History of World War II*. The Military Press, 1979.

Berlin, Robert H., "United States Army World War II Commanders: A Collective Biography," *The Journal of the American Military Institute*, vol. 53, no. 2 (Apr. 1989).

Bradley, Omar N., *A General's Story*. Simon and Schuster, 1983.

Bradley, Omar N., *A Soldier's Story*. Henry Holt and Company, 1951.

DuPuy, R. Ernest, *St. Vith, Lion in the Way*. Infantry Journal Press, 1950.

Eisenhower, Dwight D., *Crusade in Europe*. Doubleday & Company, Inc., 1948.

The Encyclopedia of Infantry Weapons of WWII. Bison Books, 1977.

The Fifth Infantry Division in the ETO. Prepared by the 5th Division Historical Section, Headquarters 5th Infantry Division, 1945.

Gailey, Harry, *The Liberation of Guam*. Presidio, 1988.

Jackson, W. G. F., *The Battle for Italy*. Harper and Row, 1967.

Jones, Clement Don, *Oba, the Last Samuri*. Presidio Press, 1986.

Leary, William M., ed., *We Shall Return: MacArthur's Commanders and the Defeat of Japan*. The University Press of Kentucky, 1988.

Lindhurst, Joe, *Military Collectibles*. Crescent Books, 1983.

Luvaas, Jay, ed., *Dear Miss Em: General Eichelberger's War in the Pacific, 1942-1945*. Westport, CT: Greenwood Press, 1972.

MacArthur, Douglas, *Reminiscences*. McGraw-Hill, 1964.

MacDonald, Charles B., *A Time for Trumpets*. Bantam Books, 1985.

MacDonald, John, *Great Battles of World War II*. Macmillan, 1986.

Manchester, William, *American Caesar, Douglas MacArthur*. Little Brown, 1978.

Marshall, S. L. A., *The Simon and Schuster Encyclopedia of World War II*. Simon and Schuster, 1978.

Maugeri, Franco, *From the Ashes of Disgrace*. Reynan & Hitchcock, 1948.

Military Collectibles. Salamander Books, 1983.

Mitcham, Samuel W., Jr., *Hitler's Legions: The German Army Order of Battle, World War II*. Dorset Press, 1985.

106th Infantry Division Pictorial Album. 1 September 1944.

Papuan Campaign: The Buna-Sanananda Operation. Historical Department, War Department, USA, 1945.

A Pictorial History of the United States Army. Crown Publishers, 1977.

The Red Diamond's First Fifty: A History of the 5th Infantry Division 1917-1967. Information Office, Ft. Carson, Colorado.

Sheehan, Fred, *Anzio, Epic of Bravery*. University of Oklahoma Press, 1994.

Shirer, William L., *The Rise and Fall of the Third Reich*. Simon and Schuster, 1960.

Spearhead in the West: The History of the 3rd Armored Division in World War II. Military Press, 1946.

Spector, Ronald H., *Eagle Against the Sun*. The Free Press, Macmillan, 1985.
The Story of the 106th Infantry Division. Handbook, 1946.
U.S. Military Shoulder Patches, 5th ed., Jack Britton & George Washington, Tulsa, OK, 1990.
Vaughan, Wynford, *Anzio*. Thomas, Holt, Rinehart and Winston, 1961.
The War in North Africa: Part 2, The Allied Invasion. Department of Military Artillery & Engineering, U.S. Military Academy, 1944.
Whiting, Charles, *Death of a Division*. Stein and Day, 1981.

Index
by Lori L. Daniel

Patch Identification

1st Infantry Division

II Corps

90th Infantry Division

VI Corps

27th Infantry Division

32nd Infantry Division

106th Infantry Division

7th Infantry Division

3rd Armored Division